MEDITATIONS OF THE SOUL

Devotional Readings For Serious Christians in Uncertain Times

Written by:
Reverend Don Meredith Welch

Editor:
Mr. Ray Glandon

Book Structure Technician:
ASA Publishing Company

Published by:
Christ Temple Evangelical Ministries
P.O. Box 38052
Detroit, Michigan 48238

MEDITATIONS OF THE SOUL

Copyright 2009 by Christ Temple Evangelical Ministries
Southfield, Michigan 48034

ISBN 978-0-615-36649-4; 0615-366-49x

*Dedicated
to
my parents,
my wife Linda,
our Children:
LaShawn, Andre, and Darrnell
and their mates:
Aaron, and Laurie.
Our Grandchildren:
Logan, CeLynn, Payton, and Cebrea.
In remembrance of the Reverend David E. Mitcham and all
the beloved members of our extended family.
To the faithful members of Christ Temple Ministries, for
whom it has been our most humble pleasure to serve since
November 1, 1986. With special mention to our officers:
Mr. Albert, Mrs. Sara Jackson, and Mr. Ronald Vaughn.*

*A special acknowledgement to Mr. Ray Glandon, for his
professional dedication to this project.
Sir, You are truly gifted.*

INTRODUCTION
AND
FORMULA FOR MEDITATION

Introduction

Reverend Welch is an Air Force veteran, father, husband. and grandfather. He has worked in public service as well as private and corporate business. He received his business training from the University of Detroit Mercy and his ministerial training from the Michigan Institute of the African Methodist Episcopal Church. He has made over one thousand-five hundred presentations through the preaching and teaching of God's Word. Reverend Welch was born and raised in Detroit, Michigan. He has witnessed the effects of recessions and hard times on families. He's had loved ones die from natural and violent means, and he knows firsthand the pains that life can issue to us all. Reverend Welch began his ministry in 1981 and has since given pastoral and spiritual guidance for nearly three decades. It has been within this journey that the thoughts and meditations found in this book have been written. *Meditations of the Soul* was written to give words of comfort and strength to ministers, Christian workers, and anyone going through the storms of life in uncertain times. In his service to those in hurting situations, he has formed the belief that the Words of the Lord address any and all problems that we may face. The following devotional readings are compressed versions of sermons preached by Reverend Welch to congregations over the years. It is our hope that as you read, meditate, and pray over these devotional readings, you will find peace for your day and joy for your soul that will help you transfer the love of God to others.

Formula for Meditation

This book is written in four parts with a total of forty devotional readings. The meditations take the reader from realizing our need for God to learning our purpose in God. The book was composed this way for anyone wishing to read the meditations during a season of spiritual renewal. *Meditations of the Soul* can be read by a seeker or a seasoned believer needing answers in hard times. If you wish to have a more personal relationship with God, it is suggested that you include fasting as a part of your devotional time. The following is our fasting model to give assistance to the reader during the period of devotion:

A Fasting Model

1. Begin with a prayer that outlines your purpose and reason for the fast: to seek spiritual self-development, to combat spiritual darkness, or to combat illness and promote health.

2. Select the type of fast you will engage such as a partial, normal, or absolute fast. Select the type of food or drink to be consumed and to be omitted during the fast.

3. Establish the length of your fast, such as three or twelve hours, one week, or forty days.

4. Read the meditation for the day and the full scripture text indicated for the meditation; they are listed at the beginning of each reading.

5. Find spiritually meditative music to listen to after your reading and during your meditation period.

6. Try to have a prayer partner that can encourage you during your fast.

7. Upon completion, engage in prayer and a scripture reading of praise, i.e. (Psalm 100); then enjoy your first meal of soft foods.

Index of Meditations

Section 1

OUR NEED FOR GOD

Section 2

LEARNING TO TRUST IN GOD

Section 3

OUR RELATIONSHIP WITH GOD

Section 4

OUR PURPOSE IN GOD

OUR NEED FOR GOD
I can't make it by myself.

MEDITATIONS OF THE SOUL
Devotional Reading for Serious Christians in Uncertain Times

"... we were weighted down, beyond all possible endurance.... " (Modern Language Bible).

Reading;
II Corinthians 1: 8-10

BEYOND ENDURANCE

Scripture;
II Corinthians 1:9

"We felt that we were doomed to die and saw how powerless we were to help ourselves; but that was good, for then we put everything into the Hands of God, who alone could save us, for He can even raise the dead."

Living Bible Version

As we review the past few years, we find events filled with broken dreams, sadness, troubles, and broken moments. We've seen more people unemployed or underemployed than we've seen in decades. We've seen sickness go through our ranks as if there was a plague waiting at our door steps. And the roll call of those who have gone from labor to reward grows longer each year. Looking at the past makes us ask ourselves what's next. What does the future hold for me, what can I expect to see, and what is my hope? Will there be new plateaus reached, new dreams realized, or is there new pain waiting around the corner? Life tells us that we can expect to see some of the same personal highs and lows this year that we've seen in the past. There will be days of joy and days of sadness. Days of sunshine and days of darkness. Death will come to the doors of the rich and the poor. Our question is, when life's mysteries become overwhelming - whom do we turn to for hope? Paul's answer is found in verse nine, when he says: *"We should not trust in ourselves, but in God which raised the dead; ..."* This is the Easter message, the message that God can raise you from death and the depths of life's circumstances because He has raised Jesus from the dead. The answer from our text is to trust in Him who can even raise you from the dead.

The letter of II Corinthians is a letter written by Paul thanking the church for listening to his message. The past year had been a year of much torment, distress, and heartaches for Paul, to the point that he was even in fear for his life. But, somehow Paul was still able to give thanks and praise to God, even after the year he had to endure. The Bible says he had strained relationships with his church family. He was disrespected, rejected, lied to and misunderstood by his own people. And then his life was threatened by the authorities. Paul had gotten down so low that he said he: *".....was weighted down, beyond all possible endurance." (Modern Language Bible).* Have you ever been weighted down beyond all possible endurance? Troubled down beyond your own ability to think or move? Pressed down to the Nth degree with bills, a lack of a job, worries about family, friends, relationships and broken promises? How do you find strength when you're weighted down beyond measure - beyond all possible endurance - beyond your own strength? How do you make it when you don't know how to make it? How did Paul overcome? How did Paul survive? The answer is he remembered the Easter message, the true Easter message. For when God the Father raised Jesus from the dead, He said to all the earth, that nothing was too hard for Him. He can create life, and He can recreate life, He can take life, and He can raise life from the dead; so no matter what you face in your life today, remember, the LORD can still raise you from the dead. No matter how dark or how deep the pain may be, with Christ you can make it. If you believe that God has raised Christ, then you must also believe that God, through Christ, can raise you as well. Believe that He can and that He will raise you, whether it is a spiritual, financial, or psychological blessing that you need. Just believe! All He asks is that you trust Him. Trusting Him with even the smallest seed of faith is more than enough faith for our LORD to work for you in your life. Remember, *"He can even raise the dead."*

Prayer:

Father, take this little seed of faith that I offer to you today, watered by my tears, and let it blossom. Help me find a new faith and trust in You that allows me to see You raise me anew.

In Jesus' Name, Amen.

"... some on broken pieces of the ship..."

Reading;

Acts 27:39-44

BROKEN PIECES

Scripture;

Acts 27:44

"And the rest, some on boards, and some on broken pieces of the ship. And so if came to pass, that they escaped all safe to land."

King James Version

We watch the lives of our neighbors or friends and think that somehow we've missed the mark. Everyone else seems to be doing so much better than we're doing. They appear to have so much more, or they seem to have the newest and the latest of everything while we're just able to get through the day. They're driving the latest cars, dressing in the newest of styles, and going to the most expensive restaurants while we try to make do with last year rejects and yesterday's leftovers. Life has us feeling as if we're existing on broken pieces.

Here we read what has been called one of the most dramatic stories of shipwreck in literature. Paul is a prisoner of the Roman government; he has been arrested and jailed on false charges. In order to know the whole story, you must start at the twenty-first chapter of Acts and read through the twenty-eighth chapter. Paul came to Jerusalem to fellowship with the other Apostles. But some local Jewish non-believers, Paul's own people, started rumors about Paul before he had even arrived in the city gates. They had already stirred a mass of people against Paul. Telling them that Paul was teaching all the Jews who lived with the Gentiles to forsake the Laws of God, as given by Moses, and to follow a new teaching. When people want to harm you, when they want to really do you in, and they don't have the truth on their side, they'll go back to some dark corner and put their heads together and begin to lie about you. They'll use other people to get at you when they're not able to get to you themselves. They'll use something that's most important to that person, something that they deeply love. Then they will tell that person that you are a threat to them and to what they hold dear - and by deception or the invention of lies, your enemies will instigate and provoke good people into doing evil things. The people grabbed Paul out of the Temple and tried to kill him. If it weren't for the Roman soldiers who came to his rescue, he would have died. He was taken to the authorities to be officially charged. Paul found himself in Ceaesarea facing Governor Festus and king Agrippa, accused by the Sanhedrine Council of heretical teaching. He was placed on a ship sailing to Italy so that he would be tried in Roman courts before Caesar. While traveling, a huge storm came up that began to destroy the ship and place all the travelers in danger. Fear had overtaken everyone on board. The sailors, in an effort to save

7

themselves, were ready to jump ship and kill the prisoners. Verse twenty says it this way: "... *when neither sun nor stars in many days appeared, and no small tempest lay on us, all hope that we should be saved was then taken away.*"

Have you ever been at a point in life where there seems to be no signs of hope in nature or in man. Have you ever been to a place that made you feel so broken that nothing could save you or keep you from falling completely apart? This is where the men of the ship stood at this moment. How did they make it, how did they survive? When we read verses twenty-two through twenty-five, we can hear Paul speaking to them of his faith in God. Here Paul stands up and tells the men, "Fear Not because an angel of the God I serve, stood by me and said, 'the ship will be lost, but we will all live.' And I believe in the God I serve. The question for you today is, Do you truly believe in the God you serve? Do you really trust His word; for God has said in Isaiah 43:2 *"When thou passest through the waters, I will be with thee: and through the rivers, they shall not over flow thee:"* And He comforts us in Hebrews 13:5 saying,"...*I will never leave you nor forsake you."* The Bible says that the centurion who trusted Paul gave the command for all the men who were able to swim to be the first in the water. Then verse forty-four reads: *"And the rest, some on boards, and some on broken pieces of the ship. And so it came to pass, that they escaped all safe to land."* Trust in the God you serve the God who made man from the dust of the earth, divided night from day with the words, "Let there be ... " Hold fast to His Word and He will take you safely to dry land, even if you're only holding on to broken pieces.

Prayer:

LORD, show me how to hold on to my broken pieces while I trust in You. Give me the strength to wait on You as Your Spirit leads me safely to dry land.

In the Name of Jesus, Amen.

"...thou art Mine..."

Reading;
Isaiah 43:1-3a

THOU ART MINE

Scripture;
Isaiah 43: 1

"But now thus saith the LORD that created thee, O Jacob, and He that formed thee, O Israel, Fear not: for I have redeemed thee, I have called thee by thy name; thou art Mine."

King James Version

The roller coaster of life often makes us feel lost, confused, sick, or lonely. We find ourselves continually searching for that something in life that brings order and peace to our souls. During the lowest moments, life itself seems to be one long tragedy after another. And the pains of life can come on us in what seems like a daily drama. Each and every day there's something new, and we begin to feel like Shakespeare when he said that life, "...is a tale told by an idiot, full of sound and fury Signifying nothing." (I)

We so often place all our hopes and dreams in our education, job, loved ones, or ourselves. When those dreams and hopes fall, our loved ones fail us, or our education proves not to be enough, we become crushed beyond expression, too weak to be lifted, and too hurt to be helped. Life can be filled with despair, and despair can bring on disillusionment, anger, bitterness, and depression. We live in that delicate balance of life and death, crying out for guidance and leadership but often unable to find what we seek.

When life has brought you greater pain than you can bear and the skies continue to rain on you each day, God is still saying, *"Fear Not,* you may get wet, but you won't drown. Turn it over to Me, and I'll carry you through." When fire comes into your life: your marriage seems strained, your children have changed, you've lost your job, and you don't even understand yourself, God is still saying, *"Fear Not,* you may feel the heat, but I won't let you get burnt. Turn it over to Me, and I'll carry you through."

I've been in the fires of life: I've seen my Grandfather and Aunt murdered. I've seen people try to steal what was mine and hurt my family, too. I've felt the heat and thought I was about to burn. When my daughter missed a plane that crashed in January of 1997, I felt the heat. When a speeding car missed my oldest son and killed the family in the car next to him, I saw the flames. When my youngest grandson was operated on at the age of five days and my youngest son was in intensive care, I felt the water and got wet, too. But I also saw God! He took the heat away before I was burned. He took the water away before I drowned. Each day I continue to see God working in my life and the lives of others; so if you don't have a personal relationship with Him, let me introduce you to my God. For He is "El Shaddai," the Almighty, All Sufficient

11

One, the God who is more than enough, and I can say I know Him personally.

Prayer:

LORD, today someone is saying I can't make it. They have not turned all their cares over to You. Let this be the day that they begin to trust You and to learn about You. Let this be the day that they realize that they need to know You. Let this be the day that they see their own insufficiencies, and then, open their souls to be filled by Your Spirit, which is more than sufficient for our lives.

In Jesus' Name, Amen.

Note: (l) Shakespeare: Macbeth V,v

"...being justified by faith, we have peace with God ..."

Reading;
Romans 5:1-21

WHY WE NEED HIM

Scripture;
Romans 5: 1-2

"Therefore being justified by faith we have peace with God through our Lord Jesus Christ; (2) By whom also we have access by faith into this grace wherein we stand, and rejoice in hope of the Glory of God."

King James Version

The book of Romans, written by Paul, reminds us of the importance of our faith in Christ. Paul begins in the first chapter reflecting on man's desire to please only himself and to live by his lust for life, serving his own gods of selfish, unrighteous pleasures. Paul tells us that because of this, God has allowed mankind to destroy itself: mind, body and soul, when we choose to serve other gods and turn our backs on Him. Everyday we look at the news it becomes evident that we have chosen to leave God out of our plans. To those whom we look to for leadership we find are often in more need of direction than we are ourselves. Teenage shootings, murders in our schools, little children being shot in their homes, all the

13

foolishness of the streets tell us that our values are in need of serious correction. These examples show us that we have fallen far short of God's Mark for our lives. The word "sin" in the New Testament Greek writings means to "miss the mark," not to hit the target. We as individuals may occasionally miss the mark, but when we as a nation continue to promote life styles that "miss the mark," then something must be done. It's obvious that if we fail to change our ways, the destruction of our society and family structure will follow.

Paul goes on in the second chapter to explain that God gave man the Mosaic Laws so that we would understand that man's righteousness falls far short of God's Righteousness. Paul seeks to make us understand that the law wasn't given to man to bring peace to man, but to make us aware of God's Standards for life. The law can not and will not save us, but it will compare our deeds to God's Goals for living. Everything within us leads us to the understanding that we need God. We need to have God direct our lives; we need to have God control our lives. This is more than a superficial need to be met by traditional ceremonial activities; it is a deeper cognitive need, a need that is internally generated, desiring to be met at the most esoteric points of life. In other words, we want God to meet us in the midnights and the mornings of our lives, in the sunshine and the rainy days of our lives-and it can't be done without a personal touch from on high.

What Paul is telling us in chapters three through five is that we can not save ourselves. We couldn't in the past, and we can't in the future. Only God can save us, through Christ Only God can save us from living in sin, from the control of sin, and from the penalty of sin, which is eternal death. Only God can save us from our sins. Because we have chosen to worship other gods, chosen to follow our own mind's desires, chosen to do our own thing and leave God out of our plans altogether, Paul continues to say that it is only because of the Grace of God and our faith in Christ that we can be saved. Not because we've been good, or because of the things we say, or where we live. Salvation is not based on who we know, or how much we make, or on how fine we dress. We're saved by faith in Christ and Christ alone.

It is God's Grace that forgives us of our sins, justifies us (takes away the guilty), and redeems us from eternal death. Faith in His birth, death, and resurrection. Faith in His Power to save, faith in His Power to forgive. That is why we are saved. That's why we need Him. That's why we can say: *"Therefore being justified by faith we have peace with God ...."* The question for each of us today is, where is our faith, is it in the God who made us or in the gods that we have made for ourselves?

Prayer:

Thank You Father for Your Son Jesus! We thank You for His Obedience to You and Your Grace that allows us a second chance to have a relationship with You. Today Father, we acknowledge that we need You, and we finally understand why, Today Father, we praise You, and we understand why. Today Father, we come to You, and we understand why. Today

15

Father, we declare You to be our only God. Help us to know You, so that we may help others understand why.

In Jesus' Name, Amen

"...*That all the earth may know that there is a God in Israel*"

Reading;

1 Samuel 17: 45-46

THERE IS A GOD

Scripture;

1 Samuel 17:46

"This day will the LORD deliver thee into mine hand; and I will smite thee, and take thine head from thee; and I will give the carcasses of the host of the Philistines this day unto the fowls of the air, and to the wild beasts of the earth; that all the earth may know that there is a God in Israel."

King James Version

Often we have committed ourselves to a task with expectations of great success and astonishing accomplishments. Once the task was undertaken we suddenly found that we were overwhelmed by the obstacles that were before us. Our well laid plans began to lack foresight and concreteness, and the task that we felt we could quickly master, began to master us. This is when we begin to see our lives in terms of our pluses and our minuses, our abilities and our inabilities. Our fears begin to take over, leaving us feeling empty and alone. It is this fear of failure that keeps us from challenging life's obstacles; it keeps us from fulfilling our commitments and realizing our goals. As Christians, our commitment is totally unto God, which means that our goals are greater than our fears and our burdens are not experienced by us alone. God never leaves us without resources, nor on our own. Where there are rivers you cannot cross and mountains you cannot climb, God will lead you in ways that are incomprehensible to you. There is no height too high, or depth too low, nor any width too wide that God cannot lead you over, under or around. All He asks is that you stay faithful to your commitment, so that when the battle is over, others will know, "*...that there is a God in Israel.*"

Prayer:

Father, I thank You for the knowledge of Your Faithfulness. Walk with me as I learn to be more faithful to You.

In Jesus' Name, Amen.

"Call unto Me, and I will answer thee,..."

Reading;

Jeremiah 33: 1-10

HOW TO FACE BAD TIMES

Scripture;

Jeremiah 33:3

"Call unto Me, and I will answer thee, and show thee great and mighty things, which thou knowest not."

King James Version

We look around our world today and see what most of us call bad times. We see nations racing each other for the power to destroy life, while at the same time doing very little to enhance life. Confusion in our economic plans and policies affects our financial positions and livelihoods. Businesses outsource American jobs, causing major concerns for American wage earners. We have more illegal drug use, crime, and health care concerns in America because of the distress borne by many of our people. For many, the American Dream has become an urban nightmare. The streets are filling up with desperate and devastated people, people who feel like life has written them off or given them a bad check that can't be cashed anywhere. For many, life seems more like something to struggle through rather than to live within. There is no joy, hope, or peace in the lives of many people we work or live with daily. Life can twist you in an instant, moving you from driving your new car to riding an old city bus. It's at that point that you believe that there is no one to trust, no one to help you, and no one you can call on.

In our text we find the prophet Jeremiah in a bad situation. He had been falsely imprisoned by his own people as a traitor. He was under house arrest in king Zedekiah's home. While there, the LORD tells Jeremiah that the people of Israel and Judah have broken their contract with God, and that because of their sins they would be placed in exile in Babylon. The future had to look mighty dim and mighty hopeless to Jeremiah. Here he is in jail for something he had not done, watching his people destroy themselves because they've put God last and self first. They've failed to love God with all of their heart, soul, and mind. They have revoked their contract with the only real true and living God and denied, renounced, rejected, and destroyed their agreement with Jehovah. And God Himself says that He will punish them. For Jeremiah, these were bad times. Our question today is "How do we face bad times?" How do you face tomorrow when your dreams have been shattered so many times that now you're afraid to dream again? What do you look forward to when your hopes have been stepped on and played with so many times that you've lost all hope in tomorrow?

In reading our text, it tells us that we must <u>First remain faithful</u>. While in prison the LORD came to Jeremiah to tell him that his cousin, Hanmeel, would be coming to him to ask him to purchase a field of land Hanmeel owned. (Under the Mosaic Laws, when a man was forced by his needs for money to sell part of his land, he was required to offer it first to the members of his family. This was called the right of redemption.) And just as God had said, Hanmeel came to Jeremiah to sell the land. Jeremiah purchased the land as the LORD had instructed him. After he had purchased the land and signed the book of purchase before witnesses, he placed the evidence of purchase in a pottery jar and gave it to his trusted friend, Baruch, for safe keeping. After all this was done, Jeremiah went off to a place by himself and prayed.

The second thing we do is to Call on the LORD in prayer. Jeremiah 32:16-25 describes for us the prayer of Jeremiah. He looks at his situation and the punishment facing his nation and people and sees only bad times; so he asks God Why. The LORD first answers Jeremiah in verse 27 of Chapter 32 and says, *"Behold, I am the LORD, the God of all flesh: is there any thing too hard for me?"* and God answered a second time in verse 3 of Chapter 33 saying, *"Call unto Me, and I will answer thee, and show thee great and mighty things, which thou knowest not."* Then God tells Jeremiah the plans He has for Israel and Judah; they will be punished now, but at an appointed time God will bring them back to this place. Then *"... they shall be my people and I will be their God.... I will make an everlasting covenant with them, that I will not (turn away from them, to do them good..." (Jeremiah 32:38-40).* God tells Jeremiah, where you now see a land that is desolate without man or beast, one day cities will be built there, and when they return unto me, I will bring them health and peace and forgive them of their sins. Shepherds shall bring sheep

21

here; people will be married here, and songs of joy and praise will be sung here. *"In those days, and at that time, will I cause the Branch of righteousness to grow up unto David; and He shall execute judgment and righteousness in the land"* *(Jeremiah 33: 16)*.

So how do we face bad times? First we're faithful. Secondly, we're prayerful. and thirdly, we believe: we believe in His promises. For God kept His promise to Jeremiah over 2000 years ago. History tells us that the land that Jeremiah purchased later became the city of Bethlehem. And in Bethlehem God did what He said He would do. For in Bethlehem God raised up the Branch of righteousness from the house of David. God placed a star in the heavens that had never shone before nor ever will again. God placed a star over Bethlehem, a star that made wise men seek Him. A star that made shepherds rejoice over Him. A star that made angels sing about Him. A star that made the king tremble because of Him. A star that said God's Word has become flesh and dwells among us. A star that said God kept His promises to man, for the Branch of righteousness has *come,* and *"...His name shall be called Wonderful, Counselor. The mighty God, The everlasting Father, The Prince of Peace. Of the increase of His Government and peace there shall be no end, upon the throne of David, and upon His Kingdom, to order it, and to establish it with judgment and with justice from henceforth even for ever ..." (Isaiah 9:6-7).*

"How do we face bad times?" What do you do when death hangs over head and your strength is almost gone? What do you do when you lose your job and you feel it's too late to train for another career? The LORD says to call Him! What do you do when the pains of life become too much for you to bear alone. The LORD says to call Him! The God who freed Paul and Silas from a jail in Thyatira ... says to call Him. The God that freed Mandela from a South African Jail and then made him the first president of their freed nation ...says to call Him. The God who showed Joshua how to bring down the walls of Jericho ...says to call Him. The God that brought down the walls that separated East Berlin from West Berlin and allowed freedom to ring once again says to call Him. *"Call unto Me, and I will answer thee, and show thee great and mighty things, which thou knowest not."*

Prayer:

LORD, thank You for being our God and answering our call. LORD, when facing our bad times, we often forget that Your Hand of Mercy and Justice is always available to Your Children. Just as You've delivered those who believed in You in the past, we know that You can and will bring us out also. Help us to always remember that You are the God in which nothing is impossible and who cares for His own.

In Jesus' Name, Amen.

"... we are troubled on every side, yet not distressed; we are perplexed, but not in despair;..."

Reading;
II Corinthians 4: I-I0

I CAN'T COPE

Scripture;
II Corinthians 4: 8

"But we have this treasure in earthen vessels, that the excellency of the power may be of God, and not of us. (8) We are troubled on every side, yet not distressed; we are perplexed, but not in despair; (9) Persecuted, but not forsaken; cast down, but not destroyed; (10) Always bearing about in the body the dying of the Lord Jesus, that the life also of Jesus might be made manifest in our body."

King James Version

We are often overwhelmed by the business of life, neither gaining any ground nor achieving any dreams. Because of this, many people have lost hope in themselves, their loved ones, neighbors, dreams and God. To them, it seems that hope is standing in the unemployment line, and opportunity is on welfare. Those things they thought would pull them through life prove to be untrue and of little security. What they thought would be the light at the end of the life's tunnel, proved to be a detour sign to destruction. Living without hope, people are fearful, nervous, and confused. They feel unworthy, defeated, and unable to cope with life, all because they have trusted in the wrong gods.

In second Corinthians, we find Paul facing the temptation of losing hope and purpose in his life. Paul's life has centered around the preaching and teaching of God's Word. Everything that Paul is about is wrapped up in his ministry. There was nothing of more importance in Paul's life than the truth of the message of Christ. Think about how Paul had to feel when *members* of his own race charged and accused him of tampering with the Word of God. Paul had spent a great deal of time suffering and sacrificing for his ministry. It was his ministry that gave him both purpose and hope in life. Paul writes the Corinthian Church to say that his faith and hope is not built on man's opinions of him but on God and the completion of the work that God had called him to do. It's not for us to be overly concerned about what others think we should be or should do when we're following God's Purpose for our lives. It's not by following the crowd, but by seeking within ourselves the seeds of the gifts, planted by God, that distinguish us from all others. It's by watering these gifts, dedicating our deeds to following His Spirit that lead us to life's greatest satisfactions and God's Endorsement with, "Well Done."

Paul, in this fourth chapter, gives what I call the personal mission statement for his ministry. He tells of the things he has renounced: (dishonesty, craftiness, and the deceitful teaching of the Word of God) and what he now lifts up high: (revealing the truth of Jesus and the knowledge of God's Glory found in Christ). It's by standing true to his mission statement and relying on the knowledge that God controls all things, even death, that Paul is able to continue his appointed mission. As you're challenged today by the opinions, labels, and remarks of others, ask yourself whose opinion matters most in your life, what others say today or what God will say tomorrow. Are you living to please others? Do you seek to fit in with someone else's agenda, or are you remaining true to the Godly mission statement designed for your life?

Prayer:

Father, keep me from falling into despair, feeling forsaken and hopeless because I've given the wrong gods power over my life. May I always place all my trust and faith in You, remaining faithful to my mission statement of life, remaining faithful to You.

In Jesus' Name, Amen.

LEARNING TO TRUST IN GOD

Increasing Our Faith

"...do thy diligence to come before winter."

Reading;
II Timothy 4:9-13 *and* 21a

COME BEFORE WINTER

Scripture;
II Timothy 4:2la

"Do thy diligence to come before winter ..."
King James Version

Winter is that time of year when we feel bitter chilling winds, see shorter days and longer nights. Spiritually, winter is a time of loss and despair, a time spent in the shadow of death. Paul writes the letter of II Timothy in his autumn season, during the fall of his life. The letter is written to give instruction and order to the church, and to prepare Timothy to receive the torch of leadership. So, first in Chapter 3, Paul tells Timothy to know the scriptures because they are *"...able to make thee wise unto salvation through faith in Christ Jesus"* (II Timothy 3:15). Secondly, he gives warnings of sufferings in Chapter 2:12 when he says *"All that will live Godly in Christ Jesus shall suffer persecutions."* He further reflects on the dangers that he had to face and the challenges that he's gone through and encourages Timothy when he says, *"God has saved him out of them all."*

Paul sits here in jail because of his service to Christ. He writes to Timothy asking him to bring some items that he needs for comfort during these dark days. Paul's call to Timothy is to come before winter because he needs his cloak for his body, his books for his mind, and the scriptures for his soul. Timothy had to come before winter because when the snow and ice come, there would be no way for him to get to Paul - It would be too late. And what I want to ask you today is, have you reached the fall season of your soul? Is winter waiting for you? Have you played through the spring and the summer of your life but failed to do what was needed to protect you from winter's snow and ice? Have you made up your mind to receive Christ's Gift and to inherit eternal life before the harsh winds of fall tell you it's almost too late? Don't wait until winter is here when your soul has become frozen and your heart is so hard that you won't know what to believe in for your soul's salvation, *"...come before winter."*

You don't have to be old to be in winter. Sickness can be your chilling wind that blows you into winter at any time, leaving you so numb that you can't think or pray. Bad habits that keep you continuously falling short of the mark can bring you into winter. When the chilling winds blow, winter comes so quickly and you don't have time to regroup. If you didn't prepare for winter, there is nothing you can do when it comes but bear the elements alone. God knew that you would need to be prepared for the harsh chilling winds that will blow into your life. God knew that you would need something for the winter of your soul, something more than a coat, something more than a book, something more than parchment, something more than your 401(k) and your CD's, something more than your degree, something better, and greater, richer, and more lasting.

The Bible says: *"God so loved the world that He gave His Only Begotten Son, that who so ever believeth in Him shall not perish but have everlasting life. For God sent not His Son into the world to condemn the world; but that the world through Him might be saved" (St John* 3: 16-17) *KJV.*

Let Christ be your cloke to warm your heart and your soul, Let Him be your book of wisdom that stimulates your mind and provides direction for your life. Let His Holy Spirit and His Word comfort you with the assurance of eternal life. *Come before winter.* Come while you still have time. Seek Him while He still can be found, because for we who believe, after every winter there is a new spring season.

Prayer:

LORD, let me not wait too long nor put off receiving the gift of Your Son Christ Jesus in my heart. Help me to come before winter.

In Jesus' Name, Amen

"*... It was good for me that I have been afflicted...*"

Reading;
Psalm 119:65-73

TO BE AFFLICTED

Scripture;
Psalm 119:71

"It was good for me that I have been afflicted, that I might learn Your Statutes."

King James Version

Have you ever been afflicted? Have you ever had something that was precious and dear to you taken away in a moment? Was there ever an event in your life that hurt you so deeply or scared you so intensely that everything that happened before and after seemed unimportant? Have you ever been afflicted? Webster says to be afflicted: "is to be dashed down, to be grieved, to be harassed, or tormented, troubled or distressed." Have you ever been put down or harassed because someone decided that this is your day and now is your turn?

If you've really been afflicted, then you must ask yourself how David can say, *"That it was good for me that I have been afflicted."* Was he mad? Let us first look at who it is that wrote these words. David was more than just a poet. He

32

had been a shepherd and a king, seeing both life's best and life's worst. He had seen folks lie to him and others trying to take his life. He lost a baby at birth, his daughter was raped, and his son had been killed. David understood trouble firsthand. David knew what affliction was all about. Yet he could say, *"It was good that I was afflicted ..."* How can David say that it was good?

Let us take a closer look at the scriptures and perhaps we can better understand David's words. In verse sixty-seven, David says, *"Before I was afflicted I went astray: But now have I kept Thy Word."* Here was a man in the winter of his life looking back and now seeing it with a wisdom that had previously escaped him before he was afflicted. Before trouble came, before he lost that, which was most sacred to him, he went astray. He went the wrong way. He failed to hear God's Voice and decided not to do God's Will. He didn't care what God said because he was having too much fun. Most of us have been there; it's the time when everything is going our way. But after you've been afflicted, the joy is gone, there's no peace, and all hope is lost. Life can never be the same again. You're no longer singing in the shower or whistling your favorite song on the street; you're crying in your bedroom and trying to stay off the streets. Yet, here sits David after he's been afflicted, writing these words, *"It was good for me that I have been afflicted that I might learn Thy Statutes."* And in this lies our lesson: It wasn't that the pain was good, it was that, in his efforts to relieve the pain, he was drawn to God's Word. He read the word of God differently, and he finally began to understand its truth. It was God's Word that healed his pain; it was God's Word that eased his fears. It was God's Word that gave him hope again. **It was God's Word that was good**, and it was good for him that he was afflicted because then he learned how to trust in God's Word, and to truly make God the Lord and Savior of his soul.

Sometimes you've got to be knocked down before you can begin to look up. Often, it's only when everything else fails that we try God; it may only be then that we sit down to learn God's Word, to study His Statutes, hear His Voice and follow His Precepts. It was good for me to be afflicted! I came to understood Your Word.

Prayer:

LORD let me seek You now before the day of affliction. I want to be strong enough and wise enough to place Your Word in my heart so that I can withstand whatever life may throw my way. Father, open my mind and heart that I might truly understand Your Word.

In Jesus' Name, Amen.

"...by every word that proceedeth out of the mouth of the LORD..."

Reading;
Deuteronomy 8: 1-6

BY HIS EVERY WORD

Scripture;
Deuteronomy 8:2-3

"And thou shalt remember all the way which the LORD thy God led thee these forty years in the wilderness, to humble thee, and to prove thee, to know what was in thine heart, whether thou wouldest keep His Commandments, or no, (3) And He humbled thee, and suffered thee to hunger, and fed thee with manna, which thou knewest not, neither did thy fathers know; that He might make thee know that man doth not live by bread only, but by every word that proceedeth out of the Mouth of the LORD doth man live."

King James Version

Deuteronomy chapter eight describes to us the second time that God tells Moses to have the children of Israel enter the Promised Land. The first time is recorded in Numbers chapter fourteen, when the people were not spiritually prepared to possess the land. So they found themselves on a forty year journey, wandering in the wilderness, as decreed by God, because they let the wrong spirit control their thinking. God had promised them this land through their forefather, Abraham, some four hundred years earlier in Genesis 15: 18-21. This was God's Promise and the dream of many generations, yet they were not spiritually prepared for the moment. How long has it been since the seed planted in your heart has seen any hope of possible fulfillment? Do you ask yourself if it still worth holding onto? Was this dream just a wish that can never come true, or was it a promise by God that now feels too out of your reach? A vision given by God will linger on your mind beyond just a day or a week; it will grab hold of you and stay in your thoughts for years and decades of time. In between your dream and its reality lays your wilderness, that time of dryness and fading hopes, the time of challenges and betrayals, the time of "may be" or "almost," when you wander aimlessly, never finding the right path that takes you to the fulfillment of the dream, your wilderness moment.

We often find ourselves asking why we have wilderness moments in life? Why does that special dream seem to escape us, and why are there so many enemies trying to keep us from realizing our dream? The forty year wilderness journey was soon to be over for the Israelites. It is now that God tells them why the time had to be endured by their people. The Bible says that while they were in the wilderness, He let them experience hunger, but God fed them with a substance they had never known. They called it "Manna." He let them travel by foot in a desert land, but God didn't let their shoes wear out or their feet swell or blister. They faced drought in the wilderness, but God gave them water from a rock when they were thirsty. Why? (1) <u>To correct their thinking</u>. The scriptures say, just as they disciplined their children, God had disciplined them to make them better. (2) <u>To know the importance of His Word</u>. God wanted them to realize that foods (or possessions) are not the most important things in life, that real life comes from obeying His Commandments and walking in His Ways. (3) <u>To test them</u>. This test is to discover their true disposition and to see if they would keep His Commandments or go back to their own ways. (4) <u>To prepare them</u>. These things were done so that they might be made ready for the blessing, the promise, and the purpose that God had spoken over Israel generations earlier. (5) <u>To humble them</u>. So that they might understand and know that it is God who gives them favor to obtain the blessing that they are about to receive.

The wilderness journey purged Israel of old slave thinking and wrong spirit and at the same time tested the spirit of the new generation. It tested the people to see if they would be faithful to God's Word. Would they walk in His Ways and follow His Commandments? Our scripture says if they are faithful, they will enter into the land: **possess**, (to occupy for generations and drive out the others) **live**: (be made whole and alive), and **multiply**: (grow and enlarge beyond measure). Our question today is, are we spiritually prepared to walk in God's Ways with full reverence for Him so that we may obtain His Blessed Promises for our lives? Are we ready to live by His Word so that the blessing from His Spirit may live, possess, and multiply in us? When the spirit in us is prepared to have

His Word guide our lives, then the LORD will open doors that no man can close and do abundantly all that we ask.

Prayer:

> *Father, today remove that which is in me that still clings to the old man and the old ways, and renew my spirit so that Your Gifts in me might be used for Your Kingdom. Teach me to be more obedient and faithful to You so that I may pass my wilderness test, so that I may live, possess, and multiply the blessings and promises You've planned for me. In all this, LORD, may my life give You glory.*

> *In Jesus' Name, Amen.*

".... O God, in the multitude of Your Mercy, Hear me in the truth of Your Salvation ..."

Reading;
Psalm 69: 13-17

THE MULTITUDE OF YOUR MERCY

Scripture;
Psalm 69: 13-14

"But as for me, my prayer is to You, O LORD, in the acceptable time; O God, in the multitude of Your Mercy, Hear me in the truth of Your Salvation. (14) Deliver me out of the mire, And let me not sink; Let me be delivered from those who hate me, And out of the deep waters."

New King James Version

Life so often seems like one big rollercoaster with all its ups and downs, twists and turns. And often the ride down lasts much longer than the ride up. Life can be overwhelming and frustrating because we are unable to grasp it in our hand and make it as we desire. We feel like the writer of James in the fourth chapter when he says: *"...you don't know what will happen tomorrow. For what is your life? It is even a vapor that appears for a little time and then vanishes away"* (James 4:14). So much of life's goodness seems to vanish like a cloud. Loved ones leave way too soon. Old age creeps up before you can turn your head, and money leaves your hand quicker than you can blink an eye. On those days you can find yourself in a state of depression covered by a cloud of sadness that refuses to go away. This is the background for our writer today. Our writer finds himself sick and at the point of death. The death he is facing is both physical and spiritual.

Physical because of his illness; he speaks to the pain and depression that he must bare. Along with this is the reality that his enemies are trying to kill him and will not stop until they've succeeded. Spiritual because everything around him has changed and will never be the same. Zion, the city that he cherishes, is in ruin. His friends don't care about him, and his family has turned their backs on him. He's even afraid to go to the synagogue because his presence may bring shame to all those who worship in the House of his God. Worse yet, our writer has waited on God so long that he's about to give up. He feels as if he's in a spiritual flood.

The Dictionary says a flood is: "An overwhelming quantity or volume of water that rises and overflows into normally dry lands." There are times in life that we've all experienced our own floods. Your flood may not be made of water, but of all the disappointments and disillusions of life that overwhelm "your" dry land. A flood may start out like a spring rain that nurtured your flowers, but it somehow turned destructive. A flood can also hit like a hurricane, inundating you with distress and trouble all at once. The circumstances of your troubles have you going in directions that you don't want to go. Your waters may have turned to a flood because of your kids, your spouse, your job, or your health. The water that was supposed to nurture you is now trying to destroy you. Those who were to guard and protect you can't be found or can't live up to their mission. You can see and feel the waters rising, killing your hopes, but all hope has not yet disappeared. Your family is falling apart, but not totally. Your finances and dreams are dying, but they're not yet dead. You can see the water rising; there seems to be no escape to higher ground, and life is overwhelming you on all sides.

Our writer can *see* the spiritual waters rising while his soul is being overwhelmed and over taken. So he says: *(1) "Save me, O God! For the waters have come up to my neck. (2) I sink in deep mire, where there is no standing; I have come into deep waters. Where the floods overflow me. (3) I am weary with my crying; my throat is dry and sore; (and) my eyes have (swollen from crying) while I wait for my God."* Have you ever been in a flood? Has life ever overwhelmed you? Our question for today is, how do I swim in a flood? How do I reach higher ground? How do I make it when I've given up on making it?

In meditating on Psalm 69, we can see in these scriptures and our writer's two prayers, just what we should not do. <u>First: Don't trust in your own piety or righteousness</u>; for he tells God of his love for the things of God, his devout life, but yet here he is in a flood. He's done everything he thinks he should do: he served in the Temple, he's sacrificed and fasted. He prayed and followed the commandments, yet here he is in a flood. You can't trust in your own righteousness. <u>Secondly: Don't trust in Man</u>. You can't place all your trust in man, because man will let you down. His friends have run from him, his own brothers and sisters have turned their backs on him. He asked for kindness, and they gave him grief. They gave him poison for food and vinegar for water. So whom do we trust? The Bible says: *"Fret not thyself because of evil doers, neither be thou envious against the workers of inquiry. (2) For they shall soon be cut down like the grass and wither as the green herb. (3) Trust in the LORD and do good, (4) Delight thy self also in the LORD, commit thy way unto the LORD, trust also in Him and He shall bring it to pass, "(Palms 37: 1-4).* Our writer takes the right step when he finally comes back to God in prayer and asks for His Mercy. Hear him in verse thirteen when he says, *"But as for me, my prayer is to You, O LORD, in the acceptable time; O God, in the multitude of Your Mercy, Hear me in the truth of Your Salvation.(14) Deliver me out of the mire, And let me not sink;..."*

Our writer understands that God can be found in the multitude of His Mercy and in the truth of His Salvation. The words of Jeremiah are still true: *"It is of the LORD's Mercies that we are not consumed, because His Compassion fail not. They are new every morning; Great is Thy Faithfulness"* (Lamentations 3:22-23). As long as you believe, trust, obey, and walk in His Word, God will walk with you and show you new mercies everyday. Turn your problems and floods over to our God, and He will show you great and mighty things that exceed your understanding.

Prayer:

Father, today I need a touch of Your Mercy in a very special way. LORD, my life has me weighted down and confused, overwhelmed and depressed, and I can't make it by myself. I need a touch from You; so I'm asking today, LORD, in the multitude of Your Mercy, to let a little mercy come down on me.

In the Name of Jesus, Amen.

"I press toward the mark..."

Reading;
Philippians 3:7-14

DON'T MISS THE MARK!

Scripture;
Philippians 3: 14

"I press toward the mark of the prize of the High Calling of God in Christ Jesus."

King James Version

When we reflect on our time here on earth, we can see our lives as a progression of steps toward goals, some great and some small. We often count our successes in life based on the achievements of such goals; dressing the way we have always wanted to dress, wearing the clothes we've always want to wear, buying the home we've always dreamed about or driving the car we have always wanted to drive. And on the day this happens, we feel as though we've reached our goals. The day the kids graduate from school. The day we get our own office with our name on the door, or the day we open up our own shop: This is the day we feel that we've reached our mark. This is the day that we've achieved the goal, obtained our destination, and hit our target. The satisfaction seems real, and the rewards seem to be so complete.

That is, until we wear out; grow out, or split out of our clothes, or until the plumbing falls apart and the furnace breaks down in our dream home. The muffler falls off the car, our job leaves town, and the store goes out of business. That's when we see that what we thought would bring us everlasting joy and peace was built on the wrong ideals. There is still within us a need for an inner peace, a fundamental hunger for something more lasting, something more permanent, and abiding. There is still a hunger that this world can't feed, a thirst that can't be quenched. This is when we see that seeking only those things in life that we can see or taste is not enough: they are inadequate, insufficient, and incomplete. They miss the mark; their satisfaction was temporary and their joy was fleeting. And this becomes the moment that we understand the words of the Apostle Paul when he said: *"For the things which are seen are temporal; but the things which are not seen are eternal "(II Corinthians 4: 18).* Somehow we've missed the mark!

Paul is writing this letter to the Christian in the city of Philippe to thank them for their concern and for their gifts to him. In his letter, Paul warns them not to trust in anyone or anything else more than Christ. For if you trust only in man and in man's way and not in God and God's Way, you'll find your heart crushed, your spirit broken, your hope stepped on and your dreams destroyed. The Bible says that at one time Paul had placed all his hopes and faith in the so called great things of his world. His life was filled with high honors. He follow the Mosaic Laws religiously - dotting every "i" and crossing every "t": he was circumcised as the law demanded;

he was educated by the best teachers; born in the best of families. He called himself a Hebrew of Hebrews. Paul trusted in his family name, his education, and his social status, to make him something special. But Paul found out that these things won't help you when the going really gets tough in life. Education can be a wonderful thing, but it really can't help you when there's no peace in your life and your heart is full of pain.

A good family name is a great honor, but a name by itself won't feed the innermost hunger of a lonely soul when its been kicked around by this worlds' madness. Only Christ can give you what your soul needs! The Bibles says, He is the way, the truth and the light. He is the bread of life when you're hungry; He's the Good Shepherd, when your soul is lost, He's the resurrection and the life when hope has died and dreams have turned to ashes. Only Christ can save you when you feel like everything is lost. He can raise you when it seems like everyone else has put you down. He can heal you, when it seems that you'll never get well. To know Christ is everything, and to know that He knows you gives you comfort that is beyond this world's concept of happiness. With a relationship in Christ, you can lose everything that this world may offer and still have joy. Paul says it this way: (7) *"But all these things that I once thought very worthwhile-now I've thrown them all away so that I can put my trust and hope in Christ alone. (8) Yes, everything else is worthless when compared with the priceless gain of knowing Christ Jesus my Lord ... I have put aside all else, counting it worth less than nothing, in order that I can have Christ, (9) and become one with Him, no longer counting* on being saved by being good enough or by obeying God's Laws, but by trusting Christ to save me; for God's way of making us right with Himself depends on faith-counting on Christ alone" (Philippians 3: 7-10, The Living Bible).

And to place anything or anyone in the place that Christ should hold in your life is to miss the mark. For the Christian, salvation and everlasting life is our goal, and through Christ, hope, joy, and peace are our rewards. He will be your joy in the midst of sorrow, your peace in the midst of the storm, your light in the times of darkness, your savior at death door, your doctor in the midst of pain. He'll be all that you'll ever need. So meditate on His Word, and pray without ceasing, and most of all, press-press toward the mark for the prize of the High Calling of God in Christ Jesus.

Prayer:

LORD, I want to have the joy that passes all understanding and the peace that surpasses this world's happiness. I want to know You and Your son Jesus, so that I may know Your Love for me.

In Jesus' Name, Amen.

"...I clung to my faith..."
(Modern Language)

Reading;
Psalm 116: 1-14

I CLUNG TO MY FAITH

Scripture;
Psalm 116: l0

"I clung to my faith, even when I said, "I am sorely afflicted.""

Modern Language

Do you ever wonder if God hears your prayers? Have you ever asked yourself if your praying was in vain? Are you wasting your time? Does God really care, or is He too busy to think about you. I'm not talking about the prayer over small concerns, "LORD, Help me get to work on time." Nor am I talking about the traditional prayers very often spoken but not really thought about, "LORD, give us this day our daily bread." I'm talking of the individual personal prayers said when all light has disappeared and only darkness exists in your life, prayers prayed when hurt can't hurt any more, when life can't be any more confusing, and hope can't be any more hopeless than it is right now. Have you ever asked yourself if God hears your prayers, your deepest, most personal, can't share with any one else prayers? Is God listening?

Our writer today has asked this very question within his soul's heart of hearts. He found himself hurting and sick, confused and lonely, wondering if God had heard his prayer and if he would ever get well. Hear him in the third and forth verses in the *Modern Language Bible,* when he said, *"The cords of death were around me; the terrors of the grave had laid hold of me, I suffered anguish and grief Then I called on the name of the LORD; "I beseech Thee, O LORD, save my life!"* *The Living Bible* says it this way, *"Death stared me in the face. I was frightened and sad. Then I cried, "LORD, save me!"* Our writer says death was staring him in the face. There's something about facing death that seems to make you get your priorities straight. You look at life with different eyes when death or the shadow of death stares you in the face. There are some moments in life that are so overwhelming and devastating that you can see death's shadow moving in on you. You can find yourself so weak that you feel you can't overcome or escape your fears, and all you can say is, "LORD Save Me." Our question is, "Where do you go when you're at the end of your hope? Who do you trust with your last ounce of faith?"

Our writer says he held on to his last degree of faith and placed it all in the LORD. Our writer turned to prayer. And after you've tried everything and everyone, it may be your time to try God. When you finally get to the moment where you have nowhere else to go, then it's time to place your trust in The Father. Trust Him with whatever portion of faith you may have remaining in your soul, but trust Him. Trust Him beyond your endurance to trust. Trust Him beyond your understanding to trust. Trust Him beyond sight or feelings; cling to whatever trust you may have left, and place it all in God. Just cling to a little faith, knowing that God is more than enough for whatever you need. He is more than enough for your troubles, your fears, your worries, your cares, your finances, your sickness, your enemies, and your hurts. He's more than enough because there is no force that can limit Him, circumstance that can restrict Him, or situation that can constrain Him.

The LORD showed our writer Grace: answered his prayer and saved his life. When God answers you, shows you that He cares and that you are important to Him, then you'll understand why our writer says in verses 1-2 "*I love the LORD, because He has heard my prayers and answered them. (2) Because He bent down to listen (to me) and I will pray as long as I have Breathe!" (Living Bible)*.

"*I Clung to my faith, even when I said "I am sorely afflicted."*

Prayer:

Father, I thank You for the little faith that I am able to cling to and for knowing that whatever I face today. You are still more than enough for me.

In Jesus' Name, Amen.

"For with God nothing shall be impossible."

Reading;
Luke 1:26-38

THOSE THINGS IMPOSSIBLE

_____

Scripture;
Luke 1:37

"For with God nothing shall be impossible."
King James Version

How often have we awakened to a new day, facing new questions and new fears that have no answer? How many times have we failed to hear the morning songs of the robins and sparrows or overlooked nature's painted masterpiece of an evening sunset? How many times have we missed the beauty in the dawning of a new day because last night's tears and yesterday's worries are still in our eyes? How many times has the fear of facing tomorrow overtaken, overwhelmed, or shattered our faith in tomorrow? How many times have we asked ourselves what we can do to fight, to battle, to conquer those things too impossible for us to defeat in our life, those habits that have been with us for so long that we can't remember not having them. That fear that hovers over our head every minute of every hour of every day that keeps us from fulfilling our true destiny is the illness that won't leave, the relationship that has lost its joy, the loneliness that won't go away - those things impossible to defeat in our lives. Luke, the writer of our text, takes on the task of showing us that when we give those things to Christ, no matter how impossible things may seem, there is nothing impossible for God. Luke was a highly educated man, a man of degrees and letters, a medical doctor with skills and faith. Luke writes **First** -to give an orderly account of the life of Christ and His Ministry. Luke wants to stress the uniqueness of this historical event: how God has revealed Himself to man as a man. **Second**-Luke speaks to us of the great number of witnesses whose names have been long forgotten, but whose deeds are no less important than those of Paul, Apollos, Peter, James, Jude, and John. Chapter one is not just an introduction of the births of Jesus and John, but a narrative on faith and prayer.

We find in chapter one examples of answered prayer, from those with different degrees of faith. We read of Zacharias, a priest from the line of Hebrew Levite Priest, a man trained in Hebrew Tradition and The Law. Zacharias was married to Elizabeth, whose own family history was from the priestly family of Aaron, (Moses own brother). The Bible says that they were seen by God as righteous believers. The Bible also tells us that they were advanced in age and had no children. Elizabeth and Zacharias represent those hard-working, well-trained, Bible-believing Christians who on the outside seem to have it all, yet there is that something that's missing. They had stature in the community; they had a great family name and history. Zacharias participated in the sacred rituals of worship in the Temple, but even for them there was that thing, that thing impossible, that one thing impossible for them to defeat or overcome, that accursed thing, The Bible says, "They had no children." In the Jewish tradition, not to have children wasn't just a point for sympathetic conversation, it was seen as a curse from God; so for Elizabeth this was an impossible thing. They had prayed day in and day out, weeks upon weeks, year after year, waiting and asking God to remove this curse from their lives, and it was still there. Then they were old, too old to have a child; it was too late, impossible. And when we look into our lives, we too have had moments when we felt that "that thing," that kept us from being complete, from being whole, from being satisfied. You may have a job, but it's not a career. You may have a house, but it's not a home. You may have a marriage, but it's not a union. And the longer you live the more impossible it seems that it will change.

So here we find Zacharias in the House of God, preparing the Temple of God for service. This was a time of hope, a time of communion, and deep faith. And at this moment of sacredness, an Angel of God appeared to Zacharias and said, *"Your prayer has been answered."* Gabriel, one of the seven spirits that stands in the Presence of God, tells Zacharias that he shall have a son and his name will be called John. Now, after all these years the answer has come, now, when it seemed that there was no way for this prayer to be answered, no way God could be listening, no evidences that God even cared. Now the answer comes. Are you now praying for, "That Thing Impossible" in your life and it seems like the answer will never come? You think about it every day and night; you meditate and mourn over it, but the answer has not yet come. How many times did you think that God had forgotten about your prayer; your prayer over that special thing, "That Thing Impossible"? The story of Zacharias and Elizabeth tells us that God answers prayers according to His timetable. God wants to get the Glory out of your life, which means God will answer your prayer when God has put all things in place and has position, time and space, spirit and flesh, the seen and the unseen in place, which is called, Karoas time, God's Time. So, today I encourage you to continue to pray according to God's Word, and trust Him all the way. God wants to work in you for an appointed time. Pray, believing not only that God "can" but that God "will" answer your prayers.

Prayer:

Father, show us how not to focus on what we see as the unfulfilled prayers of our lives; but help us to see You working out amazing wonders in our lives each day. Help us to remember that You're still in control of our lives and all that comes our way.

In Jesus' Name, Amen.

"Trust in Him at all times,..."

Reading;
Psalm 62:1-8

TRUST IN HIM AT ALL TIMES

_____

Scripture;
Psalm 62:8

"...*Trust in Him at all times, you people; Pour out your heart before Him: God is a refuge for us.*"

New King James Version

Dry places of the soul, lonely, dark, empty places of despair; with little or no hope. Hurts without any promise of relief. All you think of are yesterday's disappointments with not a glimmer of light for tomorrow - the dry places of life, where no matter how hard you struggle you just can't seem to conquer your problems. Faith - testing places, wanting places, waterless places, decaying places. And some day, at some time in your life, without warning, life will take you to a dry place.

The loss of a loved one so dear to you that it steals your will to live another day, can be a dry place. Loss of your job, or your business, or your church can be a dry place. Or, it can be the realization that the Devil is winning the war for your child's soul and you aren't able to do anything about it.

My commentaries couldn't pen down the date, city or time that David wrote these words, but I believe I know where David was living. He was in a dry place, not so much physical as it was spiritual. Dry places are where your soul thirsts, yet there is nothing to quench it. A mortal thirst can be quenched by almost anything. As long as it's wet and cold, it's all right.

But when your soul thirsts, you need something deeper and sweeter, something different and nurturing, something filling and quenching. You need waters from a pure stream and a sacred fountain because nothing else can save you or make you whole. David was in a dry place, needing to taste living waters. This was no ordinary man that found himself in a dry place. He was more than a poet that penned soul searching words. David had been a shepherd and a hero, a fugitive and a warrior, a musician and a king. He was one who had been so close to God, that it was said that he was after God's own Heart. Yet, he wandered so far away from God that he begged the LORD to, *"Restore unto me the joy of Thy Salvation"* (Palms 51:12).

So the question today is, whom have you made to be your God? Whom do you place your faith in when it really counts? Whom do you call on when you're in your dry place? David says: *Trust in Him at all times: ye people, pour out your heart before Him: God is a refuge for us.* The history of man has shown us that man has made everything from the sun to pet rocks to our bank accounts, our gods. But, whenever you place faith in anything you can see and feel you place faith in a false god, a god that can not save you, a god who can not hear or feel you, a god that can not speak to you or answer your prayers. David writes this psalm to help us realize that to place our hopes, our faith, our expectations in anything but the one true living God, opens us to a life lived only in the dry places, without any true hope of salvation. David uses this psalm to warn us about misplaced trust and misguided expectations. David uses verses nine and ten to warn us about loving power and money so much that we misuse and abuse other people. When we take a closer look at verses 3, 4, and 9, we see David telling us not to make men our God, because man can't be trusted, no matter the relationship. You can't make your husband or your wife your god. You can't make your doctor, your preacher, or your mayor your god. Only God is God. David is saying to trust in man is like trusting in a vapor, a cloud, a mist, something without foundation or sustenance. It's here one moment and gone the next.

What David wants us to understand is that we can trust the LORD our God with all our heart, and He will not let us down. Another reason we can trust Him is not only because He has the power to fix our brokenness, but verse twelve says He also has mercy. And when I'm in a dry place, I don't only need a god of power, I need a god of mercy, I need a compassionate god, one who understands me, who can feel me and care for me, and who will listen to me when I need someone to hear my hearts tears. I need a god of mercy, for a god of grace and mercy will always give me more grace than I desire and precisely what I need. And as with David, because my God has rescued and sustained my family and me time and time again, I can't help but trust Him. So today Trust in Him at all times, no matter what or who you must face in life, for God has truly proven Himself to be a refuge for all who trust in Him.

Prayer:

LORD, today teach me how to trust You more, teach me how to trust You with all my cares; the small and the large. Allow me to hide my fears in You and then to be bold enough to respond according to Your Word.

In Jesus' Name, Amen.

"Fret not thyself because of evil doers...!"

Reading;
Psalm 37

TO ENDURE IN THE FACE OF EVIL

Scripture;
Psalm 37:1-5

"Fret not thyself because of evildoers, neither be thou envious against the workers of iniquity. (2) For they shall soon be cut down like the grass and wither as the green herb." (3) Trust in the LORD and do good; ...(4) Delight thyself also in the LORD; and He shall give thee the desires of thine heart. (5) Commit thy way unto the LORD; trust also in Him; and He shall bring if to pass."

King James Version

Have you ever been the victim of an act of evil placed on you for no reason of your own? Have you ever been hurt by the foolishness of someone else? If evil has touched your life, then there has also been a change in your view of life. You can't feel as free as you once felt. You're not able to walk the streets with the same confidence that once surrounded you. With the negative stories broadcasted into our homes daily, life can become frightening. And for many the fear of living life has overtaken any thoughts of enjoying life. Life seems to be under a constant threat of danger, causing confusion, chaos, and bewilderment.

We see drug houses in many of our neighborhoods and drug addicts living on our own street. There are troubles in our schools, troubles in our homes, in Washington, our State Capitals, and our City Halls. Fears and troubles are all around us, filling us with distrust and anger. We don't feel safe sending our children to the local playground because evil has taken over our streets. And we see that those who have caused all the troubles that we endure never have to bare the pain that we go through. It seems as if they just float through life unaffected by its many pits and plunders, untouched by the many slings and arrows of life, seemingly gaining riches, power, and prestige while we fall further and further behind. It's hard to endure evil and evildoers without becoming angry or envious at what we see. Yet, this is what we are called to do. The challenge is to somehow do good in the face of evil, to work for what is right while enduring wrong.

How can we do good in the face of evil? How do we go forward when we've been violated by the evil and the wicked of this world? How do you trust when you see fear on the faces of people around you knowing that you're helpless and unable to do anything about it? How can you trust when you feel as though you've been kicked and beaten, hurt and forsaken? How can you trust when all you see tells you not to trust, but to surrender and to forget everything else? How do you endure in the face of evil? Our text gives us two principles:

first have faith in our God and not ourselves; and second; trust in the promises found in His Word.

The first principle is to have faith in our God and not ourselves: If we let our troubles look larger than our God; then our troubles will always hold us prisoner to our fears. Fear of life can imprison you; faith in God can free you; fear will bring you emptiness; faith can bring you fulfillment. Our faith is not in man, not in our employer or our teacher or our mate. Our faith is in a source greater that ourselves, one with knowledge more discerning than our own and with a love more enduring than our mother's. Our faith is in Him who is both Alpha and Omega; who is King of kings and LORD of lords; who is the Beginning and the End, and the Creator of both time and space. David says to *'Trust in the LORD and do good; ... (Psalm 37:3).*

The second principle is to trust in the promises found in His Word: Here in Psalm 37 David tells us of the faithfulness of God and what He will do for those who truly trust in Him:

"He will give you the desires and secret petitions of your heart .... The Word says *"The arms of the wicked shall be broken, but the LORD will uphold the righteous... The righteous shall not be put to shame in the time of evil; and in the days of famine they shall be satisfied ...Though you fall, you shall not be utterly cast down, for the LORD will grasp the hand of the righteous in support and uphold him .....The mouth of the righteous utters wisdom, and his tongue speaks with justice.... The LORD will not leave the righteous in the hands of the wicked But the salvation of the righteous is of the LORD; He is their Refuge and secure Stronghold in the time of trouble. And*

the LORD helps them and delivers them; He delivers them from the wicked and saves them, because they trust and take refuge in Him" *(Psalm 37: 17-40)* Amplified Bible.

We open our Bibles and we read His Words, and His Words bring us comfort and peace, strength and truth. When we trust Him and trust His Word, even when evil is all around us, we too can say like David; *"By this I know that You favor and delight in me, because my enemy does not triumph over me" (Psalm 41: 11)* Amplified Bible. Trust Him!

So when troubles come, Trust Him! When worries come, Trust Him! When pains come, Trust Him! When heartbreak and heartache come, Trust Him! When life gets too rough for you, take your cares to the LORD and Trust Him! Just pray to Him and Trust Him. Believe in Him and Trust Him! Whatever comes your way today, just Trust Him.

Prayer:

Father let this be the day we trust in You more than we trust in our fears. Remove all envy and fear of those who will not trust in You but live by their own rules. Help us to remember that their end is soon to come; they will vanish like smoke. Help us to remember that Your Promises are always faithful and true. We thank You for Your Faithfulness and Your Word.

In Jesus' Name, Amen.

"How shall we sing the LORD's Song in a strange land"

Reading;
Psalm 137: 1-6

TO SING IN A STRANGE LAND

Scripture;
Psalm 137: 3-6

"For there they that carried us away captive required of us a song; and they that wasted us required of us mirth, saying, Sing us one of the songs of Zion. (4) How shall we sing the LORD's Song in a strange land? (5) If I forget thee. O, Jerusalem, let my right hand forget her cunning. (6) If I do not remember thee, let my tongue cleave to the roof of my mouth; if I prefer not Jerusalem above my chief joy."

King James Version

Did you wake-up this morning saying to yourself, "This is not where I belong?" Have you ever felt there is no reason to smile? Do you ever feel that others are laughing at your most profound thoughts, taking what you believe to be sacred as a source of entertainment? Do you sometimes feel that the people you respect, fail to take you seriously? Have you ever seen your most constructive comments pushed aside as if they were unimportant? Then you know how it feels to be in a strange land.

Psalm 137 is a psalm of lament. Not the lament of one man, but of an entire community. The community was in exile in the land of Babylon, and the foundation of its being was in disarray. The community was in a state of confusion because their symbols of security were destroyed. Their symbols of pride, culture, and uniqueness were no longer in view. Their eyes could not see the great hills and mountains that represented home to them any longer. They did not hear the sounds or sense the aromas and fragrances that were unique to their homeland anymore. And in Psalm 137, the Hebrew people set at the side of the rivers of Babylon, missing their homeland of Jerusalem and the people that they loved. The Bible tells us that the Hebrew people had been exiled on three different occasions: the first in 722 BC; the second in the year 597 BC, when the tribe of Judah was exiled to Babylon; and the third ten years later in July of 587 BC. It was at this time during the last captivity that Psalm 137 was written.

The people of Jerusalem had been persecuted and abused, and now they found themselves at the river's edge looking at strange plants and hills in a strange land. They're breathing what seems like strange air with strange smell, being produced by strange people. And when they began to look back and remember "the what was" and compare it to the "what is," they began to weep deep tears of sadness, as they remembered special moments and special people back home. They remembered the skills they used to create, develop, and build their own homeland. When you enjoy what you do in life, when you love the work that you perform, the payment is found in the application of your skill in services to others, in the appreciation of your talents, by others. It's in knowing that others can see that there is more to you than what appears on the outside. When you love what you do, it becomes stimulating, gratifying, and self-rewarding; it gives you high self-esteem and a noble self-worth. But the Babylonian had taken the pleasure out of their day and the joy out of their living. They had destroyed their dreams and stepped on their hopes. Have you ever had your dreams stepped on because of the foolishness of someone else? Have you ever had your plans deferred because of someone's spiteful envy? Has someone ever placed pain in your life because they just didn't want you to succeed? When this happened to them, God's People began to put away their instruments and hung them in the trees. They wanted to quit.

They decided it's easier to quit and give in than to stay steadfast, unmovable, and committed. But the race is not won by the swift nor the battle by the strong; it is he who endures to the end that shall be saved. When we would rather smoke, sniff, or sip our way through life than to hold tight, believe, and fight for our rightful place in life, we're giving in to the pressure of being a child of Zion in a strange land. And here the children of Zion had lost their hope, and they were filled with despair. But worse yet, the Babylonians wanted them to sing a song of Zion. You know people like that, people who want you to give up who you are in order to be like them. The Babylonians worshipped Babel, not Jehovah, and now they were laughing because they wanted to be entertained by one of God's Songs, sung by God's People. How can they sing God's Song to these strange people in this strange land? These were the people who had killed their parents and friends, destroyed their homes and burnt down the Holy Temple of God, the people who had enslaved them. How can they sing the LORD's Song to them! The Babylonians wanted them to act like they were happy to be in the midst of this misery. In life you will find your own personal Babylon because there are people out there who want you to sing their song and dance to their tune. They'll throw pain on you and expect you to like it and to act as if nothing has happened at all. They want you to sing a Zion song in a strange land. And as People of God, we find ourselves in a strange land everyday: on our jobs, in our class rooms, on our streets, and in our neighborhoods. We find ourselves singing God's Songs to strange people.

And because of all the oppression and confusion around them, the Hebrew People somehow had forgotten about God. They had forgotten God's Power, God's Promise, and God's Presence. To forget means to cease to remember, to fail to recall, to overlook, or to disregard. <u>They cease to remember God's Power</u>. God's Power to heal them when they were sick, His Power that created both heaven and earth and all things that walk, fly, or swim. His Power that placed the stars on high. His Power to heal the brokenhearted, to set the captives free and to mend a wounded spirit. <u>They fail to remember His Presence</u>. They had forgotten that even in Babylon, God is still God. God still sees, knows and cares what happens to them. When David thought of the Omnipresence of God, he said, *"Whither shall I go from Thy Spirit? Or whither shall I flee from Thy Presence? If I ascend to heaven, Thou art there: if I made my bed in hell, behold, Thou art there. If I take* the wings of the morning, and dwell in the uttermost parts of the sea; Even there shall Thy Hand lead me, and Thy Right Hand shall hold me (Psalm 139:7-10). They overlooked and disregarded His Power, His Presence and also <u>His Promises</u>. For God said to *"...call on Me in the day of trouble and I will deliver you" (Psalm 50: 15)*. They had forgotten the Words of God spoken to Jeremiah: *(11) "For I know the thoughts that I think toward you, said the LORD, thoughts of peace, and not evil, to give you an expected end. (12) Then shall ye call upon Me, and ye shall go and pray unto Me, and I will hearken unto you. (13) And you shall seek Me, and find Me, when ye shall search for Me with all your heart" (Jeremiah* 29:11-13). They had forgotten what God spoke in Leviticus; that He will be their God and they will be His People and He will walk among them, He promises to hear your prayer before you speak. He said He'll make your enemies your footstools. He'll open doors that no man can shut and shut doors that no man can open. He said, *"Call Me and I will answer thee, and show thee great and mighty things which thou knowest not" (Jeremiah 33:3).*

This moment was also a time of testing, to see whom they really believe in as their God. The end had not yet come; the promise of the future was still alive. It was for them to hold fast to what they had already learned from God in the past, so that it will bring them through their present and future challenges also. In other words, don't forget God. Remember exile periods help transform our short-term thinking, so that we are more in line with God's long-term generational Plans. Following only our plans, doing everything our way without God, only leads to short-lived satisfaction and often to long-term pain. When the writer of the Psalm thought about God, he thought about His Power, His Presence, and His Promises, as well as what God has already done. Then our writer realized that a song of Zion is not just any song but a praising of God that should be sung anywhere, at anytime, and in any place. It's a worshiping of God for all the good things that He has done. It's for us to let the world know who is our God. It's letting the world know that there has never been a battle that our God couldn't win, a burden that our God couldn't lift, or a life He couldn't touch.

God loves you and He loves you now just the way you are; He doesn't ask you to be something you're not. All He asks is that you believe. *"... Believe that He is, and that He is a rewarder of them that diligently seek Him" (Hebrews 11:6).* So no matter how you may feel about where you are today. remember God is leading you to higher plateaus. So, I tell you today that you've got a song to sing. A Zion song to sing. A song that has the inner vision of a Stevie Wonder and Ray Charles. A song that has the beat of Quincy Jones and Kirk Franklin. A song that says, "Who we are, and Whose we are." A song that says, "I am some body, I'm special, I am a Child of the King." A Song of Zion is a song of praise and faith, a song of trust and hope. A song that says I can trust the LORD with all my hopes and all my dreams, because He's faithful.

So what is the writer saying to us today? What one thought is most important of all that has been said and written? **It is this!** "How can I forget what God has done for me?" Never forget what God has done for you. Never forget where He's brought you from. Never forget His Promise for your future. Our writer says it this way: *"If I forget thee, 0, Jerusalem, let my right hand forget her cunning. (6) If I do not remember thee, let my tongue cleave to the roof of my mouth; if I prefer not Jerusalem above my chief joy."*

Prayer:

Father. I pray for the grace to trust You more. LORD, do not let the actions of the Babylonians in my life derail me from completing my destiny in You. Let me not quit or turn back to the old ways or old friends that would confuse my journey. Let me always remember You.

In the Name of Jesus, Amen.

"...the LORD gave, and the LORD hath taken away; blessed be the Name of the LORD."

Reading;
Job 1:19-21

THE COST OF OUR FAITH

Scripture;
Job 1:20-21

"Then Job arose, and rent his mantle, and shaved his head, and fell down upon the ground, and worshipped. (21) And said, Naked came I out of my mother's womb, and naked shall I return thither: the LORD gave, and the LORD hath taken away; blessed be the Name of the LORD."

King James Version

Job has become the symbol of all human suffering and tragedy. Anyone who has suffered an undeserved, adverse, situation in his life has thought about the life of Job. His is not the story of anyone man or anyone group of men: Job represents mankind. No matter what your cultural background or political attachments, Job and his suffering can or will someday represent you. The verses of Job are often quoted because the spirit of his words so completely encompass that of every man during the times of painful, confusing thoughts.

The book of Job is considered one of the world's greatest writings. This poem is placed with other great works such as Dante's, *Divine Comedy* and Milton's, *Paradise Lost.* The writing of Job takes on more than just the thoughts of a man with great patience; the book is meant to make us look at a more fundamental issue than that of deserved verses undeserved suffering. It makes us take seriously the cost of holding on to our faith. What cost are we willing to pay in order to obtain the highest levels of faith.

Faith at its highest levels stands firmly rooted in a belief derived from our personal experiences with the Divine: experiences which have deepened our relationships and knowledge of God. Our faith is often tested, sometimes shaken and questioned; but with every experience of disappointment and suffering in life, we entrench ourselves just a little deeper and hold on to God's Hand just a little tighter. It's often the sufferings of life that make us look beyond ourselves and seek to truly see God. The poem of Job was not written so much to tell us about the patience of a man, but it was written to show us the Divinity of God and the humanity of man. It shows us the relationship of God the Creator, to man: God's Creation. It ties together for us the two theological concepts of grace and faith in such a way that we each see a little of Job in us and a little of us in Job. If you've ever had to face rough moments or had to choke down some bitter pills in your life you've spent a moment in time on Job's bed of affliction and found yourself questioning God and His reasoning in your life. You may have asked yourself how much must I bear; how long must I bear it; how do I keep holding on; what price must I pay?

Chapter one of Job begins by telling us that Job was an upright man, one who feared (or respected) God and turned away from evil. Under the Hebrew meanings, this tell us that Job was a man of high morality and integrity. He was a man that was both physically and mentally healthy, who followed all of God's Laws and served him faithfully. He was esteemed by his neighbors and thought of as a man who could do no wrong. Yet, Job still was not immuned from suffering.

The Bible tells us in this poem that there was a day when the Angels of God came before Him to give their reports. It also tells us that even Satan came. God asked Satan, for his report. Satan said that he had been on his rounds, walking up and down, to and fro on the earth seeing whom he could tempt. God asked, Have you considered my servant, Job, there is none like him. He fears God and turns away from evil. Satan acknowledged that Job feared God. God had given him riches beyond measure and blessed everything that Job touched. God had protected him and his family, and his possessions, built a hedge around him from harm. Satan proposed that he be allowed to take away Job's wealth, curse his property, touch him and bring him pain, and then see what Job does. God agreed, Satan could touch his things, but not Job's life. The Devil has to ask permission from God before he can bring unwarranted harm into your life. You see, Satan can't do any more to you than what God will allow him to do.

We've all read about or heard about the unmerited suffering of Job many times; but allow me to place it in a more contemporary format:

Your car has been repossessed, and your home is going in to foreclosure. Your job called and said that a new company has just bought the plant where you work and you've been replaced by a robot. Your summer house was set on fire. Your motor home was driven away last night. The doctor said your son has AIDS. Your unmarried daughter is expecting. You're showing the first signs of colon cancer, and both your health and homeowners insurance were cancelled yesterday. Now you understand how Job feels. And when Job saw what life had dealt him and how adversity exploded all over him, the Bible says that he didn't curse God; rather, he worshipped God. He tore his clothes, and cried, and moaned, but he didn't curse God. He fell down on his face, but he didn't curse God. He groveled and wept, but he didn't curse God. The Bible said he blessed God. I know it's difficult to praise God when life jumps on you. I know it's hard to have faith in tomorrow when today was so dark. I know it's hard to bless God when it seems like God has cursed you. But if you can somehow praise Him for the good in the midst of the bad. If you can whisper a prayer when your heart is hurting, your mind is running away from you, and adversity is knocking you down, then you'll be able to see the stars shine in the darkest parts of the night. You'll be able to reach the calm hiding place that is located within the eye of every storm. You'll be able to find the place where the wicked cease from troubling and the weary are at rest. You'll be able to see that weeping may endure for a night but, joy does come in the morning. If you can pay the cost for your faith. If you will keep on praying, working for, and waiting on God, you will reach new levels of faith in Christ, and He will be with you in the midst of every storm. You'll be able to see that God is still in control and that even through your troubles; God is working for your good. Romans Chapter, 8 verse 28 says, *"And we know that all things work together for good to them that love God, to them who are called according to His Purpose."*

So the question is: Was the cost worth paying? Is the cost ever worth paying? And the answer is always, "Yes." For in Chapter 42, the Bible says that Satan was defeated; and the LORD blessed Job in his latter days, more than in his beginning days. The Bible says that somehow Job was able to push aside his pain and pray for his foolish friends; and after Job prayed for his friends, the LORD gave Job twice as much as he had before. His family and friends came to comfort him and eat with him. They gave Job money and gold rings. God gave Job fourteen thousand sheep, six thousand camels, two thousand oxen, and one thousand asses. Job had seven new children and lived another one hundred and forty years. And such is the development of our faith: we endure hardship; then we learn to trust and step closer to God. When we faithfully continue to serve and pray God enlarges our blessings and multiplies our victories. And as life goes on, the process starts all over again, each time raising us to new levels of faith and relationships in Christ.

Prayer:

Father, we thank You for holding us up and covering us during the storms of life. Help us to remember that when life touches us with a storm, that it's only a test meant to strengthen our faith in You. LORD, please, show us how to live the life of a faithful servant.

In Jesus' Name, Amen.

OUR RELATIONSHIP WITH GOD

To know Him so that we may know ourselves.

"...Which of you shall have a friend, and shall go unto him at midnight..."

Reading;
Luke 11:1-13

A FRIEND AT MIDNIGHT

Scripture;
Luke 11:8

"I say unto you, Though he will not rise and give him, because he is his friend, yet because of his importunity he will rise and give him as many as he needeth."

King James Version

We find Christ explaining to us the importance of prayer in Luke, Chapter 11. <u>Jesus first teaches us how to pray</u>, then shows us why we pray. In verses 2-4, He gives us the most sacred prayer ever written, that of the LORD's Prayer, to <u>first show us how to pray</u>. Prayer is our communication with God. It is an outpouring of thoughts, cares, and desires from the created to the creator. Prayer is an avenue in which man can find reconciliation between himself and his maker.

<u>Secondly we're taught why we pray</u>. Jesus asks us to imagine ourselves at midnight going to one friend asking for help for a second friend. Midnight is when you feel your

deepest pains. Your aches, ache more, and your distress and fears are deeper at midnight. It's a time that you can hear your every thought and feel your every hurt. Sickness, betrayal, or deceit may be your midnight. Your job or your child, your mate or your parent maybe your midnight.

And when it's midnight in your life, you'll need a friend, and not just any friend. You'll need a special friend, one you can rely on, who will stop whatever he's doing to listen to your request. At midnight, you need the friend that Proverbs say, *"sticketh closer than a brother"* (Proverbs 18:34). One who the Apostle, Peter, says in I Peter Chapter 5, verse 7 that you can cast all your cares on, because He cares for you. One who can take you to the other side of your pain. One that's knows your heart at midnight, perhaps your family and so-call friends have left and no one else wants to be bother with you. So, at "your" midnight hour you better have a relationship with someone you can call on, someone who neither sleeps nor slumbers. Whatever may be in your heart today that caused you to have your midnight, know that you have a friend in Christ. The Love of Christ is without any conditions. His Love is for all: young, old, crippled, crazy, blue, purple, or green. God just loves, and He loves you just as you are today. This passage is saying to you, that when midnight comes into your life and it seem as though you have nothing, you still have Christ: He is your Friend at Midnight. Knock at His door. He will answer and open it to you. Ask and He will hear you. Come to Christ and find what you need.

Prayer:

Thank You Father, for being our friend as well as our God. Help us trust You more, so we can have that relationship which only comes with a true friendship. LORD, it's in understanding our position in You that gives us the boldness to introduce You to others and the strength to rest on Your Word.

In Jesus ' Name, Amen.

"One thing have I desired of the LORD..."

Reading;

Psalm 27

I WANT TO KNOW YOU BETTER

Scripture;

Psalm 27:4

"One thing have I desired of the LORD, that will I seek after; that I may dwell in the House of the LORD all the days of my life, to behold the beauty of the LORD, and to enquire in His Temple."

King James Version

Psalm 27 is one of the most beloved and well-read of all scriptures. Here David speaks of high praise, and thanksgiving for God because of the favor shown him by our LORD. The Psalm speaks to God as the Unchanging Helper and Constant Supplier of our needs. Reading through the lines we can not help but see ourselves somewhere between the poetic prayer and the prose of these lines.

Hear David describe his troublers and tormenters: liars and false witnesses, people who will get in court and make up tales just to bring you down. Enemies and adversaries on every hand, trying to hold him back from fulfilling his purpose in God. David says in verse 10, *"[What, would have become of me] had I not believed that I would see the LORD's Goodness in the land of the living!" (AMP)*. David is saying, His heart would have fainted. He would have given up, melted, fallen down and fallen apart. But God showed him mercy, hid him from dangers both seen and unseen. God took up his cause, made his enemies stumble and fall down, gave him confidence in his future, provided a secret place of shelter, and allowed him to raise his head once again. Furthermore, God placed him higher than his enemies, who were trying to pull him under their feet. David knows that Jehovah is the LORD of his salvation and the LORD of his strength, as well as the Light in his darkness. God quieted the lies of his adversaries, taught him not to fear or be afraid of men and what they would try to do to him. David could not help but want to know God better. To have the LORD teach, lead, prepare, and help David see with new eyes and a new mind and heart. David wanted to see the LORD, to dwell with Him, to live and be in His Presence, as well as, learn of Him and inquire and meditate on His Ways. David understood what the LORD had done and how He had always been with him in good times and bad, that it was the LORD's Hand that guided him. David was convinced and persuaded beyond all doubt that he needed the LORD because he couldn't fight life's battles alone. He couldn't win life's struggles by himself. David continued seeking to know the LORD searching His Word so that he may hear the LORD and to feel His Presence around him. Let this be the day that you reflect and remember all the different occasions that the

LORD led you to victories over your enemies, protected you from danger, healed your illnesses, and lifted you from moments of despair. Make a list. Then search His Word for a greater understanding of why God loves and cares for you, and what it means to be a Child of God. Seek to know Him for yourself.

Prayer:

LORD, thank You for covering my back! Thank You for thinking about me, even when I failed to think about You. Teach me, show me Your Ways, and inspire my heart to want to know You more. LORD, help me know You so that I might know myself.

In Jesus' Name, Amen.

"Restore unto me the joy of Thy Salvation;..."

Reading;
Psalm 51:10-17

THE THRILL IS GONE

Scripture;
Psalm 51:12

"Restore unto me the joy of Thy Salvations; and uphold me with Thy Free Spirit."

King James Version

This is one of the greatest prayers recorded in Biblical History, connected to one of the greatest stories in history. Here king David prays and pleads to God to forgive him for what he's done. It's not an open prayer, or a general prayer speaking of a multitude of errors. It's a prayer that seeks a very special forgiveness, a prayer delivered in deep fear, with a sincere knowledge and desire to ask God to remove a stain that even king David can not erase. This one sin has built a wall between him and his God that even the Israelite army can't break down.

When someone has hurt you that you trusted completely, it is almost impossible to restore that same level of trust. When you've been hurt because of something that was no fault of your own or because of some one's selfish desire, it's difficult to bring back the joy of friendship. David wronged God, and because of that, there was no joy in David's life: no peace and no beauty in life. For David, the thrill for life was gone.

So David Prays. He prays a heartfelt prayer of deep contrition, knowing that there is no other way to mend the wrong that he has done. Have you ever done something that you wish you could take back, created a hurt that couldn't be removed, spoken words you wish you hadn't, carelessly done something because you felt you'd never be caught, something you felt was hidden deep in the dark corner of yesterday. If somehow, by chance this has happened in your life, and you want to remove this stain, follow David's example. Take it to the LORD in prayer. Pray that your life might be changed; pray that you might know the joy of your salvation; pray for forgiveness; pray for a new spirit and a new mind; pray for a new heart and a new relationship. The Bible says that God is faithful to forgive us of our sins. Pray that He might touch you with His Spirit of Inner Peace.

David had slept with another man's wife, (Bathsheba), and then tried to hide his deed by having her husband, (Uriah), killed in battle. The day came when David began to understand that his sins weren't just against men but against God. He not only trespassed against his neighbor and lied to his people, but he also trespassed against God. That's why David prayed in Chapter 51, verse 4 saying, *"against Thee, and Thee only have I sinned and done this evil in Thy Sight."* Once David realized what he has done, he prayed this prayer, sincerely wanting to mend the breech that his deed created. David knew that no one could fix this relationship but God. So he said in Chapter 51, verse 10, *"Create in me a clean heart, O God: and renew a right spirit in me...Restore unto me the joy of Your Salvation;..."*

If your life today is heavy because of something you've done that your spirit will not let you forget, come to our LORD through His Son, Jesus, in prayer. If you come to Him with a broken spirit and heart, He will give you a fresh start. He will forgive and show you mercy because it's His Nature to always have mercy. The Bible says in 1 John Chapter 2, verses 1-2, *"... We have an advocate with the Father, Jesus Christ the Righteous: And He is the propitiation for our sins: and not for ours only, but also for the sins of the whole world."* Thank God for Jesus, for we are only forgiven because of God the Father's Love for His Son. When we come to Him in prayer, He hears Christ speaking for us and forgives because His Son requests forgiveness on our behalf. Thank God for Jesus.

Prayer:

Father, we come today thanking You for Your Mercy and Your Son. LORD, You know the thoughts that hold on to our minds, that will not leave our souls because of what we've done. Today LORD, we are asking in Your Son's Holy Name that You forgive us, cleanse us, and bring back to us the joy of our relationship *with You.*

In Jesus' Name, Amen.

"Now faith is..."

Reading;
Hebrews 10:38-39, 11:1-6

THINGS NOT SEEN

Scripture;
Hebrews 11:1

"Now faith is the substance of things hoped for, the evidence of things not seen."

King James Version

The eleventh chapter of Hebrews is one of the literary masterpieces of the Bible and especially of the New Testament. The Sermon on the Mount, The LORD's Prayer, Romans the eighth chapter, I Corinthians the thirteenth chapter, Revelations the twenty first chapter and Hebrews the eleventh chapter are classic writings of the New Testament. The words, *"Now faith is the substance of things hoped for, the evidence of things not seen."* rings of such great truth that they echo within our minds and hearts over and over again. Those words and our belief that get us through the sometimes overwhelming pressures of today.

It has become more and more real that for many of us it's our faith in an unseen God that gives us courage to get up in the morning. If we didn't have faith in tomorrow, then we would fall back into yesterday. And to fall back into yesterday is to stop believing in the Promises of God and how He is working in our lives, that our lives somehow don't matter, that our dreams can never come true. Hebrews was written to Jewish Christians to strengthen them in their resolve to serve God and to tell them not to fall back into old patterns of beliefs. Paul reminds them of the ancestors that walked this journey far before they were born. He starts in Chapter 11 verse 3, by telling them that it's their faith that helps them understand that it was God who created the Heavens and the Earth and framed the Universe. He states that by faith Abel was found more righteous than Cain, that by faith Noah built an ark and saved his family while the rest of the world laughed and call him crazy. The Bible says by faith they crossed the Red Sea on dry ground and that by faith the walls of Jericho fell down, that by faith they conquered kingdoms, overcame injustice, shut the mouths of lions, won wars, escaped death, and endured hardships. Some were tortured, some were beaten, some imprisoned, some stoned, and others were killed. But it was by faith, faith in an unseen tomorrow that they were able to have the victories that we read about and preach about today.

We all have our load to carry, and we all have our pains to bear. We all have moments of sadness, disappointments, and unfulfilled dreams. And you'll soon find out in life that you need a source of hope outside yourself, or you will collapse under life's weight If you fail to have a source of hope that is greater than yourself, that is stronger, wiser, and more knowledgeable than yourself, then you will lose hope and fall back into despair. You will give up, give in, faint, fall by the wayside, and quit. And if your life today is without an anchor, if you don't have a savior who is closer than a brother, loves and cares for you, then my friend, you are truly on your own.

To live without a savior is to live without hope, and a life without hope is a life that has no dreams. It's a life where everyday is cloudy and the sun never shines. It's a life that has no hope and can see no future for yesterday is always better than today and tomorrow. But what Paul is saying to us today is that a life in Christ is a life that has great hopes and great expectations. A life in Christ is a life that has an unnatural faith in a supernatural God. A life in Christ doesn't mean that we won't have pain, but it does mean that Christ will ease all our pain and dry all our tears. It doesn't mean that we won't thirst, but it does mean that with Christ our thirst shall be quenched and our hunger shall be satisfied.

Once you know Him for yourself, you know that no matter how hard the task, no matter how rough the road, no matter how salty the tears, The LORD will make a way somehow. With each battle and each victory in life you learn that you can count on Jesus; you learn that you can trust in Him. You can trust Him as your Friend and Savior; you can trust Him as your LORD of lords and King of kings. Scripture says. *"Thou wilt keep him in perfect peace whose mind is stayed on Thee; because he trusteth in Thee' (Isa.* 26:3). When we keep our hearts, our minds, and our every thought on Him, we are able to have faith in things not seen. We can trust Him because we know that when no one else cares, He cares; when no one else sees, He sees; when no one else understands, He understands, and when no one else can, God can!

Prayer:

LORD, give us faith that looks beyond the seen and believes beyond the tangible. Most of all, Father, give us faith that allows us to trust in tomorrow as we Trust in You.

In Jesus' Name, Amen.

"Rejoice in the LORD..."

Reading;
Philippians 4: 1-7

THE JOY OF THANKSGIVING

Scripture;
Philippians 4: 6-7

"Be anxious for nothing, but in everything by prayer and supplication, with thanksgiving, let your requests be made known to God. (7) and the Peace of God, which surpasses all understanding, will guard your hearts and minds through Christ Jesus ..."

New King James Version

There are moments in life that require you and me to pause and reflect upon our personal course in life and make adjustments for the journey ahead. Thanksgiving Day is always such a day. It is a day that demands that we ask the question, "What do I have to be thankful for this year?" If we look at the past year and review our successes and our failures, our achievements and our downfalls, our struggles, and our days of comfort, we will see that life is a mysterious thing. For some of us the past year was bright and sunny, filled with great joy.

Others will find that the past year was anything but glorious. Some of us have lost loved ones, jobs, and long hoped for dreams. Some have lost their faith and hope in the future. And because of this, many look at these days not with thanksgiving but with regrets and disillusionment. For them life seems like a joke and they're the punch line.

After carefully reading Philippians and reflecting upon the writing, we may be able to see what Paul is trying to teach us. If you search back over time and remember where you came from and what you had to go through to get to where you are today, you'll understand that you didn't make it by yourself. In the midst of your trials and tribulations, your pain and your tears, no matter how impossible it seemed, God was there. He was there lifting you and speaking to you. And it was His Voice in the middle of the night giving you strength to face a new morning. Paul is writing this letter in the middle of what had to be one of the most troubling times of his life. Paul is in Rome imprisoned for his faith, a situation that would give him a right to break down, be depressed, and lose faith. But Paul says, "To Rejoice ..." How can a man who finds himself imprisoned for political motives still find reasons for joy and thanksgiving? It doesn't make sense. When we think about it, all of us have been imprisoned at sometime by some of life's situations, when life has been so overwhelming and overpowering it seems that our very existence has been placed on hold and that our spirit to live has been defeated. So, how can Paul rejoice while he's in prison?

The answer is found when you can view life the way Paul did. When you are able to see that in life, it's not the up's but the downs, not the highs but the lows, that made you strong, then you, too, can say, "Rejoice!" It wasn't the sunny days but those lonely nights that taught you how to trust in God. When you begin to see that through all your hurts and pains, trials and tribulations, God was there, helping and protecting you, touching and healing you. When you think about how God has answered your prayers, opened doors and blessed you in ways that you can't describe, then you, too, can pray with thanksgiving and know the Peace of God, which passes all understanding.

So, if He has healed you, then thank Him. If He's lifted you, thank Him. If He has touched you, thank Him. If He's been there to bless you when no one else would hear or help you, then you should thank God for bringing you through. So before you cook that turkey or watch your TV, don't forget to give the LORD a hand clap of praise and a shout of thanksgiving. Don't forget to rejoice in the LORD on Thanksgiving Day and everyday of your life. Know that the same God that was with you in your glory days will be with you in your dark days, too.

Prayer:

LORD, help me to rejoice in all situations. Help me to have a new vision which allows me to see You in all things in life, both good and bad Then, LORD, help me to know that whatever I may face today, You won't allow me to face life alone.

In Jesus' Name, Amen.

"Then I understood their end."

Reading;
Psalm 73: 1-18 and 28

NOW I UNDERSTAND

Scripture;
Psalm 73:28

"But it is good for me to draw near to God: I have put my trust in the LORD GOD, That I may declare all Your Works."
New King James Version

How many times have we asked ourselves whether it's worth it? Are our struggles to do the right thing or our efforts to walk the narrow path worth the cost? Or maybe the real question is "Whether we're foolish to try to do good in such an evil world." Should I push my beliefs aside and follow the crowd? Should I give up and give out in order to be more of what others say I should be?

I feel that most people seek, and desire the finer things in life, and to be a Christian doesn't mean that we should be continually poor and ragged, crying and complaining. The Promises of God to us are far more wonderful than to have us stepped on and kicked around all our lives. But there are times when we look around and see things as they really are and wonder why life doesn't match our desires. We see evil being lifted up in every corner of our lives. It seems as if they who do the most wrong receive the greatest praise and rewards. And we ask ourselves what we're doing wrong that we're down here and they're up there.

Our psalmist is writing from this same prospective today. He sees the wealth and riches, the opulence and affluence of the wicked and wonders why God doesn't strike them dead. They're able to go to the finest of restaurants and sit in the best seats. They sit up front with the leaders of government, commerce, and church. The writer said that after he looked around and thought about it, he wanted to go over to their side.

The Living Bible says it like this:

"I came so close to the edge of the cliff. My feet were slipping and I was almost gone. For I was envious of the prosperity of the arrogant and wicked." He said, *...Their lives seem so smooth-without troubles. They wear their arrogance on them in everything they do."* The writer goes on to say that what hurts even more is that everyone else is going along with the program, praising them and speaking of their greatness.

Sometimes we think God doesn't see what's happening, because if He did, something would change. But I've learned that God gives all of us time to think, to look at ourselves and the mess that we've created. He often gives us chance after chance to change, to turn our lives around, and to get right with Him. God is a patient God, but there is that moment that forces God to say, "Enough is enough, that's it! If you won 't change, I'll change things for you." For when God is ready to make things change, you better believe that everything will change. When God is ready, the wicked will cease from troubling and the weary will be at rest, and justice will roll like waters and righteousness like a mighty stream. Don't fear; God does see what is happening, and He won't wait forever before He makes a change.

Our writer needed somewhere special to go in order to find the answer to the dilemma he found himself in; for he was about to give-in and fall. And when you find yourself in need of an answer that is beyond that given in the text books you've read; then you also need somewhere special to go, somewhere greater than the universities and colleges, somewhere friendlier than the parties and the bars. You'll need to go somewhere that the God of Peace and Healing can be found, where after weeping has endured for a night, joy will come with the morning light. You'll need to go to God's House, to the Sanctuary of the LORD, and the Synagogue of Faith. The writer says only after meditating in God's House was he able to understand. Sometimes we need to go and just sit and be still in God's House. We need to quiet ourselves to find the answers we search for in our LORD's House. Our writer understood that the wicked are like a bad dream to God, and that they will be wiped out, destroyed in a moment in a twinkling of an eye, they shall be gone and casted into the eternal fires of Hell. And now, after the writer reflects on all that he has learned and seen, he says in Chapter 73 verse 28 that:"...*It is good for me to draw near to God; I have put my trust in the LORD...*" This is the message of the psalm. Our relationship is built through the Agape Love of Christ for us and our responding love for our God. Our relationship gives us confidence that God cares, loves us, and is watching over us every day. For that, we must be thankful. Because of that we must praise, glorify, and bless Him!

In Chapter 73 verse 22, the psalmist's mind has been opened, and his eyes are now able to see. He said that he was a fool, he was ignorant like a dumb animal before the LORD. He didn't realize that it was the LORD who had been with him every step of the way. God held him in the middle of His Hand, guided him, and gave him counsel and direction. And he now knows that when time is no more, it will be the LORD who will take him up, receive him, and give him a new home in glory.

And then in Chapter 73 verse 25, he says, *"Whom have I in heaven but You? And there is none upon the earth that I desire beside You... For God is the strength of my heart and my portion forever and ever and ever!"* When we go in prayer and meditate on God's Word, we get closer to God. There we will find greater wonders and even greater truths. In moments of darkness we'll be able to see shades and shadows, and then, eventually, the LORD will show us His Light. It is then that we will be able to understand God's Love for us and see what God has prepared for a life lived in Him.

Prayer:

LORD help us understand Your Will, Your Way, and Your Love. Help us to see that no matter what others may have or do, there is nothing more wonderful than our relationship with You.

In Jesus' Name, Amen.

"I will say of the LORD, HE is my Refuge..."

Reading;
Psalm 91: 1-6

THE 91st PSALM

Scripture;
Psalm 91:2

"I will say of the LORD, He is my Refuge and my Fortress: my God; in Him will I trust."

King James Version

Psalm 91 is a psalm of praise and trust. The writer is speaking of a profound faith wrapped in a very simple message, that they who dwell, they who abide, they who stay, (not those who jump in and out but they who believe and trust) shall know God as their Fortress and their Refuge, as their Sustainer and Savior, as well as their Shelter and Sanctuary. Life on this earth can be dangerous, and you find out very early in life that you can't trust everyone that you meet. You learn over time to protect yourself from being too open, too kind, or too helpful. Often people will take advantage of you and cause you to feel foolish and naive. But to live life trusting only in yourself is extremely dangerous. In order to make it through life, you must learn how to trust someone; you just can't make it by yourself.

This is what the writer has learned and what he's saying to us today: there are traps out there waiting to swallow you up and take you away. There are people who want to control you, to tell you where to go and when to go there, They want you to bow down to them because they think they have power over you. They neither care about you nor care about the people you care about. It's all about them and how to get you to serve them. So, when the psalmist talks about the snare of the fowler, the noisome pestilence, the terror of the night and the arrows of the day, he's talking about the mess you've got to go through just to make it from noon day to midnight, from morning sunrise to evening sunset. There are people who envy you and want to bring you down, who pretend to be your friend in order to steal what you have, who tell lies on you, gossip about you, who want to hold you down and keep you from achieving more than what they have.

And if you think you can trust in Old Grand Dad to save you from lies, messes, diseases, and devils, you better think again because you're trusting in the wrong God. You' re trusting in a God that starts dying as soon as the bottle is empty and who is dead when the buzz wears off. When pain gets so deep that you don't know if your coming or going, moving or standing still, praying to your dope dealer won't help you. Talking to Jim Beam or Old Crowe won't save you. A joint won't get you high enough, and a pill won't last long enough to get you through. You've got to be in tune with a

God whose power is deeper than a bottle, higher than a joint, wiser than a psychic, and more compassionate than crack. You need to know the Most High God, the Almighty King, the Everlasting Lord. You need to seek a personal relationship with the Father. Once you begin your personal relationship with our God seek to live and dwell in His Word, He will become your Refuge from the storms of life. He will be your Fortress of safety from the liars and demons who want to destroy what you stand for in life. He will cover you with His Truth and Shield you from the traps that others set for you. Seek Him; have a personal relationship with Him; know Him as your God, and He will give angels charge over you. He will hold you in His powerful Right Hand.

But let us understand that what the psalmist is speaking about is deeper than what most of us see in this scripture. For he's not just talking about our earthly comfort or our mortal frame. What he is referring to is of more consequence than nicks and bruises, hurt feelings and occasional pains. He's talking about the God who is able to keep your very soul from death, a God who can keep evil from destroying your life and eternal soul, a God who can protect you not only here under the confines of time but also beyond time, when time is no more and eternity begins. He will protect you if you will just dwell in His Shadows and abide under His Wings. Seek to know God, and see who He really is. Know Him as your Sustainer and Savior. Know Him as the Forgiver of your sins and the Sanctuary of your soul. Make time now to dwell in the Secret Place of the Most High, and you will forever abide under the Shadow of the Almighty. And He will truly become your LORD and Refuge.

Prayer:

LORD, I want to know You in a very personal way. I want to feel the joy of my salvation and understand the peace that can only come from Your Spirit. Help me see You for all that You are. Let me know Your Love.

In Jesus' Name. Amen.

"...we have access by faith into this grace wherein we stand,..."

Reading;
Romans 5: 1-8

LIVING ON THE EDGE

Scripture;
Romans 5: 3-5

"And not only so, but we glory in tribulations also: knowing that tribulation worketh patience; (4) And patience, experience; and experience, hope: (5) And hope maketh not ashamed; because the Love of God is shed abroad in our hearts by the Holy Ghost which is given unto us."

King James Version

The thoughts of our minds often take imaginary trips down the corridors of life's journey, trips which often lead us into some very frightening episodes. We have all awakened from these dreams feeling our heart beating faster, our minds racing out of control, taking us to, the edge of life, not knowing if we would survive or not. But, as the moment of extreme danger arrived, we somehow were pulled out; we were rescued, we were saved, we somehow woke up. How much like life are our dreams, or maybe I should say how much like our dreams are our lives. If we really think back, we can see how over and over again life has taken us to the edge. Dangers, seen and unseen, have lurked all around us, and we didn't always know how we were going to be rescued. Financial dangers, domestic dangers, unemployment, and ill health, have stared us in the face, and we didn't know how we were going to make it. But somehow, someway, the incredible, the unbelievable, the inconceivable happened. Somehow we were saved. We were freed from the horrors that had beset us, and liberated from the fear that imprisoned us. Somehow we woke up. There was nothing we did that contributed to our rescue, and no super hero came to our aid, there was a deeper dimension. The rescuer who led us to our liberation was of a more powerful source than a comic book character.

This rescuer who freed us has powers beyond our comprehension and understanding. When we finally wake up, we can see, we can understand, and we know who it is that saves us from our fears. When we finally wake up, we clearly see our weaknesses and frailties, our vulnerabilities and inabilities. We see that it's God who controls the lives of mankind, not we alone. It's God who is making the impossible, possible and the ugly beautiful again, mending the brokenhearted, and setting our souls free. We live on the edge. Our lives are being controlled by our fears, fears that twist and toss the souls, that drain us and cause such pain that death may seem more pleasing than life.

So, how do we live beyond "Life on the edge"? How do we gain enough faith to face a life impacted by an innumerable amount of fears? Paul gives us our answer in Chapter 5 of Romans. He says it's our faith in the compassionate power of Christ and the Loving Spirit of God that gives us our peace. It's when we strive to live in His Presence and surrender our will: our heart, mind, and soul unto God's will, that we can find that peace that will overcome our fears. Then we can walk by faith and not by sight and trust beyond any earthly reason to trust. For in His Presence life's dangers have no strength to overpower us, for in His Presence is perfect love, and *"Perfect Love casteth out fear ... " (I John 4:18).*

The deeper our relationship with the Father, the deeper His Presence will be in us, and the greater His peace becomes in us. That's why Paul said that we glory in tribulation, because with each trial that life brings us, we learn to lean on the LORD just that much more. And our relationship becomes a little deeper; our fears become fewer, and our peace and faith becomes more enduring. When God becomes personal in our lives, He becomes Jehovah-Shalom, "The Lord of Peace" all through our lives; He becomes Jehoshooah (Joshua), "The LORD who saves" all through our lives; He becomes the LORD who heals, who protects, who will comfort us all through our lives.

When God becomes personal to us, Christianity stops being a religion; it becomes a relationship. God becomes our Savior and Redeemer. We become His children and the object of His Love, and we no longer live a life on the edge, controlled by overwhelming fears.

Prayer:

LORD, let me know Your Presence today; right now! Let me find the peace that is beyond understanding; let me know that I am Your Child and the object of Your Love. LORD, come into my heart and revive my spirit again.

In Jesus' Name, Amen.

"*...and there was no water for the host, and for the cattle...*"

Reading;
II Kings 3: 4-20

NO WATER IN THE WILDERNESS

Scripture;
II Kings 3: 17-18

"For thus saith the LORD, Ye shall not see wind, neither shall ye see rain; yet that valley shall be filled with water, that ye may drink, both ye, and your cattle, and your beasts. (18) And this is but a light thing in the sight of the LORD: He will deliver the Moabites also into your hand."

King James Version

Today we see a story that calls us to look deeper at ourselves and our true relationship with God. We find in the third chapter of II Kings the story of two kings. The first king is, king Jehoram, whose name means "Jehovah is exalted" but whose life said something totally difference. He was the son of king Ahab and his wife Jezebel. The same Jezebel that introduced Baal worshiping to the land of Israel. And because of that, the nation of Israel began to worship a god other than the God who had brought their fathers out of the House of Bondage. Jezebel's name brings thoughts of immorality and wickedness in high places, and Jehoram was her son.

And the Bible says; *"And he wrought evil in the sight of the LORD; but not like his father and like his mother; for he put away the image of Baal that his father made."* (3) *"Nevertheless he cleaved unto the sins of Jeroboam the son of Nebat, which made Israel to sin; he departed not therefrom" (11 Kings 3:2-3).* In short, he made a superficial change, but on the inside he never made a spiritual change. Do you ever wonder what your epitaph will say about you? Will it say that you put on a good show on the outside but failed to live up to the advertising behind closed doors? Or will it say: Here lies a true miracle of God, saved by His Grace, washed in His Blood, made whole by His Love, a blessing to all he touched.

The second king is, king Jehoshaphat; the fourth king of Judah after the division of Solomon's kingdom. The Bible depicts him as a good king serving the LORD Jehovah. He increased the strength of his walled cities, forts, army, and business enterprises and reorganized his nation's judicial system. He sent Levites and priests to teach in the cities of Judah, expounding the Book of the Law of the LORD. We have two kings, each descendants of Abraham, having a different relationship with God. In this journey we call "life," our relationship with God will make all the difference in "our" outlook at the world. Our relationship will determine how we look at life and all its challenges. Do you look at life with God, seeing opportunities for new victories, or do you fight life without God, often being overwhelmed by your fears?

The background today speaks of a time when the king of Moab stopped paying tribute taxes to Israel when king Ahab died: tributes of 100,000 sheep and the wool of 100,000 rams each *year*. This was a significant amount of tribute and diminished the treasury of Israel substantially. To us, Moab represents the great losses of our lives, not ordinary losses or hurts, but deep losses and deep hurts. The death of a mother or father, of a husband or wife, the child lost on drugs, the loss of your dream job: These losses leave you so broken that you feel that you will never be whole again. Moab is that deep hurt that weakens you to your bone and knocks you to your knees. It makes you wonder why me? Have you ever had a Moab moment in your life, or are you going through a Moab moment right now?

Jehoram decided to restore his losses using his own ways. He called on Jehoshaphat, the king of Judah, and then he called on the king of Edom. Three kings, three nations, and their armies going against one; surely there was no way that they could lose. With Jehoram's might, cunning, and connection, he felt that victory was well in hand. The three armies journeyed through the wilderness to destroy Moab. But after seven days, the Bible says there was *"no water for the host, and for the cattle that follow them."* There was no water in the wilderness, and they believed they were facing death. And in Chapter 3 verse 10, king Jehoram said, *"The Lord called us here to deliver us to our enemies."* And our question for today is, "How do you handle your dry wilderness? What do you do when there is no water in your wilderness?

You're in the wilderness when you go to a place of salvation, but there is no one there to help you, or when the third doctor says, "I can't cure you," or when even your part-time job lets you go. You're in the wilderness when it looks like all hope is gone, that there is no future for you because what you thought would quench your thirst, nurture your soul, and feed your spirit, was dry, barren and empty.

Jehoram trusted in the wrong people and wrong god and left the God of Abraham, Isaac, and Jacob out of his equation. So, how do you handle your dry wilderness moments? Do you do like Jehoram, or do you follow the example of king Jehoshaphat? The Bible says in Chapter 3 verse 11, that king Jehoshaphat said, *"Is there not here a prophet of the LORD, that we may inquire of the LORD by him?"* How do you make it when there is no water in the wilderness? According to our text you: R,H,P,M, and O: You (R) Remember the God you serve. (H) Humble yourself before Him. (P) Pray to Him. (M) Meditate on Him, and then, you (O) Obey Him.

First: (**R**), Remember in Chapter 3 verse II, king Jehoshaphat remembers and acknowledges the God he serves. Verse twelve shows us the second principle, to (**H**) Humble ourselves before Him. The three royal leaders humbled themselves and went down to the preacher house to find an answer. The three kings were able to put away egos and reputations to meet with a lowly preacher in order to hear from God. Thirdly, we (**P**) Pray. II Chronicles 7: 14 says that when we humble ourselves and pray before the LORD, He will hear, forgive, and heal us. The three kings went to Elisha to ask him to pray for a word from the LORD to deliver them from the king of Moab. Verse fifteen says Elisha asked for a minstrel so that he may meditate while he prayed. The Bible said, *"When the minstrel played ... the Hand of the LORD came* *upon him."* Our forth principle is to learn how to **(M)** Meditate You may not have your own private minstrel, but you can meditate on a song, a song that will touch the heavens, break your depression and make an angel fly down to hear your music. And after you've followed the first four principles and you've heard the answer; the fifth, and most important principle is to:

(O) Obey the Will of God. I Samuel 15:22 says *"To obey is better than sacrifice ..."* The first four principles mean nothing if you fail to execute the fifth one. It's when you obey God's Word that He fulfills His Promise. That is when you're able to see that what was impossible for you to fix, overcome, or defeat *"is but a light thing in the sight of the LORD."*

Elisha tells the kings to dig ditches in the valley, that they won't see the rain or hear the wind but the valley will be filled with water, that they'll have enough water for themselves, their armies, and their cattle, but even greater than that, God will deliver Moab into their hands. It didn't sound smart to do what Elisha said, but they obeyed anyway. Sometimes what God asks you to do may not make sense to you, but all He asks is to trust Him. If you do your part, just believe that God will surely do the rest. Why would God save us from our Moab and wilderness moments? It's because of our relationship with Him. He loves us and has given us His Favor. *Psalms 5:12 says: "For thou LORD will bless the righteous; with favour wilt thou compass him as with a shield."* God's Favour is when He gives you what everyone else says you don't deserve. God's Favour is when your enemies outnumber and outgun you, but you achieve the victory anyhow. And we who are called the children of God have our Father's Favour!

The Bible says the valley was filled with water and the three kings and their armies were able to both drink and water their cattle. Because the Moab king didn't hear rain, he thought the ditches were pools of blood and felt that the three armies had killed each other. So he ordered the troops to go down and finish the job. The Bible says that when his army arrived, the Israelite army beat them all the way back to Moab and then destroyed their cities.

So whatever your Moab moment or your wilderness experience may be, remember *"this is but a light thing in the Sight of the LORD"* Whatever may be hurting you today, turn it over to the LORD; then R,H,P,M, and O. He can change your mind, bind your demons, make your enemies your footstool, and bring water to your wilderness. When we place Him first and follow His Will, whatever the fear we face maybe it's, ... *but a light thing in the sight of the LORD".*

Prayer:

Father, Thank You for Your Favour. LORD, help me to remember that when my problems seem too daunting for me to handle, they're but a light thing in Your Hands. I ask, believing in faith and accepting with full confidence, that You've already transformed my circumstance by Your Spirit.

In Jesus' Name, Amen.

"I know thy works, and tribulation, and poverty, (but thou art rich)..."

Reading;

Revelation 2: 8-11

I KNOW YOU

Scripture;

Revelation 2: 9-11

"I know thy works, and tribulation, and poverty, (but thou art rich) ...(10) Fear none of those things which thou shalt suffer: ... be thou faithful unto death, and I will give thee a crown of life."

King James Version

You've taken on the challenge of standing for right and righteousness in a world that declares this to be the antithesis to its thinking. You've set your path on a straight course of travel for a higher level of achievement, making decisions based on your sacred beliefs. You now find that those you felt would understand "the why" of your thinking, question your every thought. The people who said they knew you best, in actuality, understood you the least. You wonder why they can't see the things with the same vision you possesses. It makes you think that your ideas are too small and your actions a waste of precious time. You begin to see that the people you felt would be your greatest support, need support themselves-from you. Not just casual support, but a deeper, almost clinical level of support that can only be given by you.

What do you do when reality deflates the storybook fantasy you once held dear? What words can counteract the feelings of shame that says your best efforts just aren't good enough? Whom do you listen to when even you question your thoughts. These are the times that demand we look beyond the people we can touch and see and get in touch with the God we can not see.

The book of Revelation gives us a great understanding of how God views His Church. In the first three chapters we find John writing to the seven churches of Asia with words from Christ. He writes to Ephesus, Smyrna, Pergamos, Thyatira, Sardis, Philadelphia, and Laodicia: seven churches, each with a different character of devotion. John writes both to praise and discipline them. He gives praise to those who have stood true, and He disciplines them where they failed to be strong. Three received both praise and discipline, and three received only discipline. Smyrna is the only church that received only words of praise and encouragement. Smyrna stood well under pressure and sufferings unlike the other six. Founded in the twelfth century B.C., Smyrna was a beautiful city with its own library, theater, and sports arena. It was so rich that it made its own coins and currency.

Smyrna had also built a temple to an emperor, an edifice for the worship of a man who felt he was god. In Smyrna, the emperor would have all your land and possessions taken from you if you didn't worship him. You couldn't work or live where you wanted if you didn't worship the emperor. I've learned in life that to crown someone emperor over our lives is to make them more influential than God. Emperors, (great and small) want to run your life and everything you do. They want to tell you when to get up and when to lie down, when to eat and how to eat, what to read and when to read it, to move only when they say to move, and to breathe when they say to breathe. Smyrna had an emperor, and the emperor was angry at the Church of Smyrna.

So Christ had John write these words in Chapter 2 verse 9, *"I know thy works, tribulation and poverty (but thou art rich)....."* In other words, Christ is saying, I see, and I know the deeds you've performed and the faithfulness you've shown. I know you! I see you! And because I know you I've prepared a special blessing just for you. I have a covenant with you, and as you have been faithful, so shall I be faithful to you. Because I know you, I will allow you to see problems solved in ways no man can understand. I will open doors that no man can shut and shut doors that no man can open. *"No weapon formed against you shall prosper; and every tongue that raises against you in judgment you shall condemn" (Isa. 54:17). Blessed shalt thou be when thou comest in, and blessed shalt thou be when thou goest out. ... (8) The LORD shall command blessing upon thee in thy storehouses, and in all that thou settest thine hand unto; and He shall bless thee in the land which the LORD thy God giveth thee" (Deuteronomy 28:6-8).* All because I know you.

Jesus also said in Chapter 2 of Revelation that He knows of those who say they are Jews and are not, but are of the synagogue of Satan. He knows of those who pretend to be a part of the family of God, who pretend to be of the Church of Jesus Christ, but are not. He knows who they are and what they're trying to do. He knows the lies they've spoken and how they are trying to push the Church at Smyrna to change. Christ said to fear none of the things you may suffer, but be thou faithful unto death, and He will give you the crown of life. For He, Jehovah -Shammah "The God Who is Present" and El Roi "The God Who Sees and Cares" will bless them with a crown of life. Not the emperor, because he just doesn't understand; not the bishop, because he's too busy; not the mayor nor the governor because they are too lost. But only Christ can give us the crown of life. Christ is saying He knows you; so trust Him. When fears come and hope is fading, trust Him! When tears come and pain won't leave and you don't know which way to turn, trust Him.

What is the lesson from the Church of Smyrna? **First, be strong**: If you're going to be a soldier for Christ, be prepared to suffer for righteousness sake because there are emperors, demons, and devils out there who want to hurt and control you. But fear not what they may try to do, be thou faithful until death, no matter what may happen. God will take care of you; God will make a way somehow. **Secondly, be faithful**: Follow the Word of God and turn not from it to the right or to the left, but meditate on it both day and night, and you shall make your way prosperous. **Thirdly, Remember**: Remember who you are and whose you are. Trust in Him who will not fail you. Trust in Him who knew you before you knew yourself, who knew your name before you had a name, who knows your dreams and your failures, your fears, your thoughts, and the secrets of your heart. Trust in Him who says: I see you; I know you; I care for you. He will hear your prayers, satisfy your needs, give to you when you ask, open to you when you knock, and receive you when you call.

Prayer:

LORD, teach me how to have a better relationship with You. Teach me to serve You. Teach me to hear Your Voice and to follow Your Word with joy. Teach me to be more of what You have designed me to be for Your Kingdom.

In Jesus' Name, Amen.

"Cast thy burden upon the LORD, and He shall sustain thee:
He shall never suffer the righteous to be moved."

Reading;
Psalm 55

TO ESCAPE THE STORM

Scripture;
Psalm 55: 4-8

"My heart is sore pained within me: and the terrors of death are fallen upon me. (5) Fearfulness and trembling are come upon me, and horror hath overwhelmed me. (6) And I said, Oh that I had wings like a dove! for then would I flyaway, and be at rest. (7) Lo, then would I wander far off, and remain in the wilderness. (8) I would hasten my escape from the windy storm and tempest"

King James Version

The fifty-fifth Psalm is within the second division of the Psalms (Psalms 42-72) where God is referred to as Elohim, "The Almighty God." David approaches God today as his Almighty God. There are sometimes in life that you need God to be more than just your healer or protector; you need Him to be your Almighty God. Life will crush, overwhelm, or cripple you so deeply that you can find yourself in need of more than just a physician or a psychologist. There are days that the

119

regular portion of God just won't do. You find yourself in need of the extra large portion, the jumbo, overflowing size of God: "The Almighty God" size. And today David is in a place where he needs an extra large portion of God. Listen to him speak of all that is in his heart, the pressures that life has placed on him. Read the entire chapter and see what David sees so that you may know how David feels. David sees his enemies denigrate him; he sees lies being told on him. David witnesses his life being threatened and his name being slandered. In the city that he loves, he watches troubles and strife grow every day; leaders make corrupt deals; the rich and the wicked oppress the poor and the weak. He finds himself in the midst of a storm, a storm of confusion and pain blowing against him, trying to pull him under and destroy everything that he has believed.

But David's greatest pain and deepest hurt is not in the ruins of his city or the threats on his life, but the storm of storms and the heartache of heartaches, is the betrayal of one he called a friend. Storms come into all our lives, some great and some small; but one day there is that certain something that becomes "The Storm." It's not just any storm; not just any sickness or loss, not just any hurt or pain, but "The Storm." Cancer attacks your colon, and that becomes "The Storm." You lose your mother; your child faces a life changing operation; your marriage breaks up: and each becomes "The Storm." For David, this was "The Storm" The friend that was more than an acquaintance, he was a guide, an equal, one he walked with to the synagogue to worship and praise the LORD. He knew David like no one else. The Hebrew word that is used here is

"Yada," which means "as a kin, like a brother, one of the family." David says his Yada, broke the covenant, tore up the treaty, tried to stab him in his back, and take his life. For David, this was the "The Storm," and in addition to everything else, it was too much.

The Bible says that all he could do was mourn and make a noise. He wasn't able to utter any words strong enough to make others understand how he felt. Chapter 55 verse 4, David says, *"My heart is sore pained within me: and the terrors of death are fallen upon me. (5) Fearfulness and trembling are come upon me, and horror hath overwhelmed me. (6) And I said, Oh that I had wings like a dove! for then would I fly away, and be at rest. (7) Lo, then would I wander far off, and remain in the wilderness. (8) I would hasten my escape from the windy storm and tempest" (KJV).* All the things that David had trusted in had failed him. He wanted to flee from his troubles. He wanted to run from his pain and hide from his storm. David wanted to fly away and be at rest. Have you ever wanted to fly away and be at rest? Have you ever wanted to escape the winds of your storm, move from your hurts and get away from reality? If you have, then you know how David felt. Our question for today is: How do we as Christians react on the day that "The Storm" comes into our lives? Whom do we trust when everyone we've trusted has turned their back on us and we're facing "The Storm" alone?

So, what does the fifty-fifth Psalm say to us about escaping "The Storm"? Just this: that we, the children of "The Almighty" should always remember our relationship with our God and know that whatever comes our way, God cares for

His own. David remembers and trusts in his relationship with the "The Almighty." For in Chapter 55 verses 16 and 17, David says: *"As for me, I will call upon God; and the LORD shall save me. Evening and morning, and at noon, will I pray and cry aloud: and He shall hear my voice."* David says to turn to the "The Almighty" God Elohim, and pray to Him and He will hear your heart. Pray to Him in the morning. Pray to Him in the noon hour. Pray to Him at midnight. Pray to Him all day or all night; pray to Him softly; pray to Him quietly; pray to Him standing up or sitting down. It doesn't matter how you pray; just pray to Him; He's waiting to hear your prayers and feel your heart.

After his time in prayer, David reaches the twenty second verse with a new philosophy and a new understanding. David instructs, directs, implores, and pleads with us to: *"Cast thy burden upon the LORD, and He shall sustain thee: He shall never suffer the righteous to be moved."* David now understands that even when "'The Storm" comes, God is still "The Almighty," and He shall sustain (defend, strengthen, fortify, and uphold) us no matter the circumstance.

Prayer:

Father, our Elohim, our "Almighty" God, we praise You! LORD how often has life overwhelmed us to the point of silence, where we could not find words to express ourselves even to You. Help us to remember that there is no problem or circumstance greater than Your ability to sustain us and carry us through.

In Jesus' Name, Amen.

OUR PURPOSE IN GOD

Under His Anointing

"What Shall I Render..."

Reading;
Psalm 116: 1-14

WHAT SHALL I RENDER

Scripture;
Psalm 116: 12

"What shall I render unto the LORD for all His Benefits toward me? "

King James Version

Have you ever, during the silent moments of time, asked yourself how you could repay your parents for all they've done for you. Have you ever wondered what would be proper payment for all the time and sacrifices that were given you through the years? Is there an appropriate dollar amount that can be calculated by using a prorated table of years of services? Is there a data base with values and equations that give you an amount equal to the care and love, patience and nurturing that you've received over the years? I think we all know that there is no unique amount that you can give to one who has really been a mother in all phases of motherhood or a father who has been more than a visitor. For someone who cooked, cleaned, disciplined, sung songs that made your dreams sweeter and spent their time making you think that you were the most special child on earth, how do you repay them? I've read about athletes who purchase a car or new homes, or set their parents up in business. But is that enough? Can this say to them, "debt paid in full"? I don't believe so. I don't believe there is any price or any object that we can give that can say, "debt paid in full." Some things are too precious to set a price and too elegant to be appraised by a mathematical system of numbers.

If we as children are unable to place a monetary value on the love received from our parents, then how are we able to place a price on the love and grace bestowed upon us by our God, who has been better to us than we have been to ourselves? God has given us gifts not asked for, hope unimaginable and fulfilled dreams that exceed our greatest wishes. How do we repay God for being God? Here lies our challenge for today: What do we give to God for all the blessings He has given to us? This is also the challenge faced by the psalmist, as he looks back at one of the most frightening moments of his life. He asks, *"What shall I render to the LORD for all His Benefits toward me?"* Our writer sits in deep, meditative thought, reflecting on what he has just gone through. He tells us that he was greatly afflicted, to a point of facing death itself. To be afflicted is more than just how, it's: "Am I going to make it to see tomorrow?" He found himself hurting and sick, confused and lonely, wondering if God heard his prayer and if he would ever get well. Hear the psalmist in Chapter 116 verses 3 and 4, in the Modem Language Bible, when he said: *"The cords of death were around me; the terrors of the grave had laid hold of me, I suffered anguish and grief Then I called on the name of the LORD; 'I beseech thee, O LORD, save my life!"*

When death stares at you face to face, you begin to put your priorities in order quickly. The realization that you may not see the faces of those who have brought you life's greatest joys, hear their voices, or feel the warmth of their presence again, makes everything else pale in comparison. Bills don't seem as pressing. Things we own don't seem so alluring or valuable. Arguments don't seem unsolvable or as significant when compared to being unable to share another moment with those you love. And when face to face with death, it can make you desperate, so desperate that you can listen to the wrong people and place your faith in the wrong things. Our writer was desperate, so desperate I believe, that in his haste to be cured, he relied on the wrong people and followed the wrong messages. He found out the hard way that they could not do what he needed to be done. They could not be trusted. He needed something greater than what they offered, something more fulfilling than what they presented. He needed something more lasting and cleansing, and it wasn't anywhere in sight. Man did not have what he needed, and does not have what "you" need. Although our schools are great institutions, they do not have everything you need. You need something more. Don't look to this world to do for you what only God can do! He is more than whatever you may think you need. Paul says, "*He is able to do exceeding abundantly, above all that we ask or think ..... (Eph. 3:20).* Heb. 4:16 says: *"Let us therefore come boldly unto the throne of grace, that we may obtain mercy, and find grace to help (us) in time of need."* God answers prayers! And our writer prayed - not a theologically structured five-part prayer, just a simple prayer, a sincere prayer: "LORD, save me!" And God heard his prayer. Remember, no matter what you may be going through today, you can still call on God. He may say, "Yes." He may say, "Wait, it's not time." He may say, "No, I have something better for you," but He will answer your prayer.

If you take a good look at your life and see the video of your time here on earth, I'm sure you'll see where God has answered your prayers. When we look close enough, we can see that God has been with us even in the moments that we're unaware of His Presence. He was there, and we have been the recipients of the great benefits in life. We've seen dreams fulfilled, hope renewed, and precious moments enjoyed, that without Him, would not have been possible. So how do we repay Him for all that He has done for us? Our writer says that he will pay his vows in the sanctuary, but what's more important than this is that he will offer the sacrifice of thanksgiving and call upon and praise the name of the LORD. Let us resolve to let it be known before all people that this God "is" God, and that we praise Him for everything in our lives. Let us live our lives today and all the days following with thanksgiving and in a way that gives Him glory.

Prayer:

Father, We just say thank you. We thank You and rededicate our lives to You so that others may see that it does pay to serve the LORD. We thank You for opening our eyes and for letting sad moments in life be turned into classrooms for wisdom. You didn't let our sadness overpower us, but allowed us to grow with faith in You. For this we are thankful.

In Jesus' Name, Amen.

"Arise, get thee to Zarephath..."

Reading;
1 Kings 17: 7-24

GO TO ZAREPHATH

Scripture;
1 Kings 17: 9

"Arise, get thee to Zarephath, which belongeth to Zidon, and dwell there: behold, I have commanded a widow woman there to sustain thee."

King James Version

In this reading we find that the Prophet Elijah is being cared for through the grace of God at the Brook Cherith. The Brook represented a time of shelter and covering from Elijah's enemies as well as a place of rest, from the famine suffered by Israel. Ravens brought him bread and meat both day and night while the brook supplied him with water to quench his thirst.

But in time the brook dried up, and king Ahab still wanted him dead. What do you do when your brook dries up and your enemy is trying to hunt you down and destroy your life? How do you feel when God's provisions have seemingly run out and there is no rain or water to drink? Do you trust God again? The real question is, when God directs you to go from one place of trust to a higher place of trust, do you have the faith to follow His Spirit? God tells Elijah to go to Zidon, the country where Jezebel's father was king. How do you trust Him when He tells you to go to a land that maybe more dangerous than where you are today? Can you arise and go to Zarephath? Between the Brook Cherith (the place of refreshing), and Mount Carmel (the place of (Elijah's), greatest victory), there is Zarephath. The name Zarephath means smelting or refining place. It was a place known for pottery manufacturing. We've read about the two miracles performed in this place, but we miss the real reason God had Elijah go to Zarephath. When we meditate on the writing closely we can see that before Elijah could have his Mount Carmel moment (where he defeats the four hundred and fifty prophets of Baal), he needed a time of refining in Zarephath. In Chapter 17 verses 20 and 21, he questions God because of his own fears and challenges of faith that would take him to where he had never gone before. When God answered his cry and revived the widow woman's son, Elijah knew without a doubt that God was with him.

The question for you today becomes, "Is God calling you to go to your Zarephath, so that He may prepare you for your Mount Carmel?"

Prayer:

Oh. LORD, our Father, help us to hear Your Voice when You wish to draw us from our resting place to a refining place.

Strengthen us so to yield to Your refining fires and be made ready to ascend to a new level in You.

In Jesus' Name, Amen.

"...*present your bodies a living sacrifice...*"

Reading;
Romans 12: 1-2

LORD, MAKE IT REAL

Scripture;
Romans 12: 1-2

"I beseech you therefore, brethren, by the mercies of God, that you present your bodies a living sacrifice, holy, acceptable to God, which is your reasonable service. (2) And do not be conformed to this world, but be transformed by the renewing of your mind, that you may prove what is that good and acceptable and perfect will of God."

New King James Version

Oh, how diligently we search for the meaning of life. Yet, we search not so much for a general meaning of life, as we do for the particular and specific purpose that gives meaning to our life. We reach out for what gives us our self-worth, self-esteem, and dignity. We follow the multi-lane highways of confusion, seeking an exit that leads us to the street of fulfillment. No matter what steps we take, or what moves we make, there still persists within us a hunger that can not be filled by this world's applause, awards, or trophies. There is still within us a song that says there is more to life than what I'm experiencing at this moment, more depth to its laughter, more knowledge to its thoughts, more inspiration to its emotions. Life is more profound than this. My life must have more significance, more importance, and more worthiness than this. LORD, make it real! Let me feel that my life is worth something and that my living is not in vain.

So often it's after we've tried everything in life to find fulfillment, only to come up empty, that we try God. It's moments like this that we understand that the greatest measurement of fulfillment is not quantitative but qualitative. Fulfillment is not based on what you take out of life but what you put back into life. Your purpose in life is not based on your self-fulfillment but on your self-sacrifice. It's not your dedication to duty for the sake of duty, but in the consecration of your soul and your being to live for God's Goals: to follow His Will and to live by His Precepts. Perfect fulfillment is only found by first seeking the Kingdom of God and His Righteousness, believing that only then will all our desires be added unto us.

Our text today is found in Paul's letter to the Gentiles Christians in Rome. Paul writes this letter as an introduction of himself to his Roman brothers. But, not only did he introduce himself, he also wrote what many consider the greatest exposition of the Gospel of Jesus Christ ever written. It was in reading Romans I: 17, in the year 1514 that Martin Luther was inspired to nail his 95 thesis on the door of the castle church at the University of Wittenburg, and thereby begin the reformation movement. In the twelfth chapter of Romans, Paul exhorts us to respond to God's Love with everything we've got, with every fiber of our being, every thought, every action, and reaction. As Christians, we should be ready to commit our names, our reputations, and our egos on the alter to God. We show our love for Christ through our service and sacrifice for others each day. Have you prayed for someone today? Did you try to help feed someone, spiritually or physically today? Have you visited the sick, clothed the needy or comforted the lonely this week? Did you help someone on your life's journey today? Did you listen to someone's problems or give them a word of encouragement? Did you make a difference in someone life?

When you enlisted in the Army of Christ, you said, you were ready to move into the untested waters of life and to wrestle with the unresolved problems of this world, believing that if Jesus called you, and cared for you, that He'll keep you, and that you would be ready to go all the way with Him. You've said you'll bear the pain supported by His Word and take the risk of making mistakes, offending people, and meeting the challenges of life, as long as Jesus is with you. God has given each of us a purpose in life that goes deeper that our own personal desires, longing, or wishes. It calls us to be involved in doing something greater and more significant than the mere act of physical labor for the sake of a paycheck alone. Our mission is the enhancement of life itself, the enrichment of humanity, and the elevation of the human spirit. This is what glorifies God, and this is what we're called to pursue. So whatever your career, whatever your profession, whatever your vocation remember that it's only by God's Grace that you are where you are and what you are today. Today's position is only a stepping stone toward tomorrow's promise.

Prayer:

LORD, show me each day how I can glorify You by the way I serve others in Your Name.

In Jesus' Name, Amen.

"And let us not be weary in well doing:..."

Reading;
Galations 6: 1-10

DO GOOD ANY HOW
(Don't get Weary)

Scripture;
Galatians 6: 9-10

"And let us not be weary in well doing: for in due season we shall reap, if we faint not. (10) As we have therefore opportunity, let us do good unto all men, especially unto them who are of the household of faith."

King James Version

We look around and see what seems to be a world out of control. Nations such as Israel, Iran, Iraq, and Afghanistan are examples. We see our communities out of control: our youth are dying, just as fast as, or faster than our elderly, and the leadership of our nation's governmental institutions are being called into question. Corporate America has been accused of cooking their books and giving a false picture of their real profits, and now asking the public taxpayer to bail them out of their troubles. Our neighbors are being killed and our neighborhoods shot up all because of misplaced values and a lack of self respect. The cost of education and health care is out of control. And as we *try* to combat the disease of the street, we see fewer victories and more defeats with even more victims.

So what is Paul saying to us today? What words of wisdom or inspiration can we conclude from our text today? What does he say to the weak from the battle of trying to do their best when others seem not to care? Paul says what David said in Psalms 27, verses 13 and 14:

"I had fainted, unless I had believed to see the goodness of the LORD in The land of the living. Wait on the LORD, be of good courage and He shall strengthen thine heart: wait I say on the LORD." So, when the battle to do good seems to be overwhelming you, and you don't know which way to turn..., wait! When dreams are delayed, hope is fading, and everything looks lost... wait! When lies about you grow faster than the truth, when others place road blocks in your way or try to make you think that you're going mad, wait on the LORD and do good anyway. Our scripture says, *"Don't get weary in well doing; for in due season we shall reap. if we faint not "* In other words, God is watching and preparing for all who believe, fight, and serve with faith, blessings beyond our earthly understanding. Due Season is when God says it's your turn and all things are prepared; it's when God has put everything in place. Due season is the day that God places your enemies as your footstool; it's the day that God uses your foes to open the same doors that they were trying to close. Due season is the day that the wicked cease from troubling, and the weary are at rest. It's the day that you see with your own eyes, that God is not mocked, and that you have reaped

what you've sown. In due season, you will possess your blessings, receive your reward, and wear your crown. Due season is coming for you; so prepare to receive your blessing- it's your turn! Don't get weary. Don't faint. Don't give up; keep on fighting. Keep on doing good; God is watching you.

So, when it doesn't seem to make any sense, do good anyway. Someone is counting on you; someone is watching, trusting, and hoping in you. Don't get weary in well doing, but wait on the LORD and do good anyway, and in due season (God's prepared time for you) you will reap if you don't faint.

Prayer:

Father God, teach me how to wait, show me how not to faint during tough times. Help me to remember that I may be the only example of Your Love that others may see today. Let my life be lived in such a way that You receive glory.

In the Name of Jesus, Amen.

"And he shook off the beast..."

Reading;

Acts 28: 1-6

HOW TO HANDLE SNAKES

Scripture;

Acts 28: 5

"And he shook off the beast into the fire, and felt no harm."

King James Version

Too often in life we're placed in bad situations not of our making. Someone spreads rumors and untruths. Something in our past may be dug up, to say to others that we haven't changed and should not be trusted. Someone may want to defame our name because he can't control how we live our lives. There are people in our lives that grab hold of us like snakes and refuse to let go. Our question today is: How do we handle snakes? When your innocent of the charges and a victim of other folks lies, how do you get rid of snakes? When you've changed your life and become a new creature in Christ, but people won't let you forget your past, how do you face your future?

We read in Acts Chapter 27 that Paul finds himself in a boat with other prisoners, being carried to Rome. The Bible tells us that the ship was caught in a tremendous winter storm. It began to leak; so the crew threw overboard spare parts and cargo in order to survive. In life, you' re often faced with occasions when you must decide to throw overboard extra weight that holds you down, keeping you back from reaching the other side. Extra weight may be a bad habit, a one-sided relationship, or fears that must be thrown overboard.

The Bible says that the men were scared and in despair, that they had lost hope and felt that death was coming at any moment. Paul stands up and tells the crew of the vision that came to him overnight. An angel told him that they would all make it to land if they would just stay with the ship. It was hit by strong winds and violent waves that tore it apart, but the men were able to reach land by swimming or by hanging on to the broken pieces of the ship. And now in Chapter 28, Paul and the others are on Melite, or modem day Malta, and something surprising happens. The people of Melite, who spoke another language and were of another race, came to their rescue. People who didn't know him and couldn't understand him came to his rescue. God has a way of sending you help from the most unlikely sources. Folks you thought didn't like or know you, can be angels in disguise. And because of this, Paul says their deed was of "no little kindness." Paul had endured troubles: he had been shipwrecked, wrongfully accused, lied about by his own people, and mentally and physically worn out. For these people, a strange people, a foreign people, to offer him a tender hand, a warm touch, and a cold drink of water, it was "no little kindness."

But in the midst of the warmth and kindness, the Bible says, up jumped a snake. I've learned in life that when you think you've gotten over all the evil that the devil can throw at you, snakes can jump up. It may be a garden snake: one full of gossip, and lies, and false tales about you. Or, it maybe a python: one that wants to smother you until you give up what is yours, so that it can steal from you. Or, it may be a viper: a poisonous snake, the worst one of them all because it wants to kill you, take your respect, and your name. It wants to take your marriage, your children, your reason for living or even your life.

If we read carefully, we can see the character of a snake because the Bible says that the viper fastened itself onto Paul's hand. Snakes wrap themselves around you. They try to get next to you and then try to get inside of you. Your snake will make you sick, swell up, choke, and be destroyed. A co-worker or your boss may be your viper. Gambling, drugs, or alcohol may be your viper. Whatever it is, whoever it is, if <u>it's not for your good</u>, **Shake it off!** Whatever his or her name is shake it off. Get rid of it, push it aside. Pray over it, and give it to Jesus. If you can't handle it because it got too close to you, shake it off and watch it get burnt in the fire. Folks who set you up - shake them off. A habit too ugly for you to break- shake it off. Fears that won't let you move or grow-shake them off! Take your hands off, and let God put his hands on. Let Him handle it, fix it, or destroy it and watch what happens.

He will either change it or He will change you. He will fix it or He will fix you. You see, God has said to, *"call on me in the times of trouble and I will show you great and mighty things that you know not" (Isa. 26:3)*. When you turn it over to God, it will not be you in the fire but the snake that's being burned. So pray, shake it off, step on it, and let God raise you up and destroy your snakes.

Prayer:

LORD, thank You today for being my Snake Handler. Take everything that's trying to fasten itself to me that is not for my good and remove it from me. Guide me so that I am able to stay focused on You and my purpose in You. Strengthen me so I trust You more each day with my snakes and my cares. And Father, help me see the good in others who may be different than me so that I don't miss the blessings sent by You through them.

In Jesus' Name, Amen.

"...but they shall not prevail against thee, for I am with thee,..."

Reading;
Jeremiah 1: 1-19

THEY CAN'T WIN

Scripture;
Jeremiah 1: 17-19

"Thou therefore gird up thy loins, and arise, and speak unto them all that I command thee: be not dismayed at their faces, lest I confound thee before them. (18) For, behold, I have made thee this day a defended city, and an iron pillar, and brazen walls against the whole land, against The kings of Judah, against the princes thereof, against the priests thereof, and against the people of the land (19) And they shall fight against thee but they shall not prevail against thee; for I am with thee, saith the LORD, to deliver thee."

King James Version

What a feeling to be invincible, to have powers that exceed all of mankind. To have the assurance that no matter how awesome the foe, how difficult the task, or how overpowering the enemy, the victory will still be yours. To be the prize fighter who knows that his opponent doesn't have a chance of victory. To be able to look at any foe dead in the eye and know that no matter how hard they try, they can' t win. Not simply to feel it, but to know it, to know without a doubt that you can't be defeated, overwhelmed or destroyed. To live with such a confidence, means that you can walk into the lion's den and not be frightened, or go into a fiery furnace without fear. It would mean that you could stand up for what you believe in and say what you feel was right, and not be afraid. All this you could do, if you knew that your enemies could not win, because you are invincible.

And to face the great evils of today, you need to feel invincible, you need something extra. You need to feel that you have both power and support so great that you can overcome this world's most evil alliances. And where does one go to purchase such power? Where can one find this reservoir of strength? Can we consume some herb, or drink some secret potion and become an invincible being? The more realistic question for us today is: How can we face our own personal lions, fires, and demonic armies and not be afraid? What can we do or take that can help us face our fears and fight our foes? In the first chapter of Jeremiah we gain insight to the answer to our question and an understanding of how he was able to fight so courageously. To Jeremiah, God was personal and transcendent; he believed that God enters into our lives with a personal touch and a caring heart. Reading Jeremiah Chapter 1 allows us to see and feel the personal intervention of God into the life of Jeremiah. At fourteen years old, God speaks to Jeremiah and calls him to the ministry. God has said that before you where conceived He knew Jeremiah. Before he was born God consecrated him to be a prophet before nations. God tells Jeremiah that his life has a purpose greater than even he can imagine. God prepared great acts for him to be a part of, great moments for him to see, great deeds for him to engage in, and great words for him to speak. God tells this fourteen year old to take His message to kings and priest, to governments, and nations.

But how can this be? He's only fourteen years old, from a small town, and he's neither rich, famous, nor well educated. How can God be speaking to him? When God's divine plan calls on you and plants a vision within your heart, the thought of it is always too astounding for you to grasp. The mere possibility of being named by God to carry out a task in His Name is too overwhelming for the imagination. When you come to the realization that God has chosen you to uses your gifts for His Purpose, your first thoughts are: "Who, me? How can this be!" And Jeremiah does the same when he replies, "I can not speak; for I am a child." How can Jeremiah, a boy of fourteen, overcome his fears and control his anxiety to be used by The Almighty. The answer is found in knowing that with God's Promotions comes God's Promises. When God charges you and promotes you to tackle a problem, He also prepares you with the tools to master the problem. God always prepares the way before you. First, God lets you know that you're not alone: because He will walk before you. God will clear the way for you, even before you begin the journey.

First comes God's Promise then His Blessed Assurance. In verse 8 of Jeremiah Chapter 1, God says: *"Be not afraid of their faces, for I am with you to deliver you."* To emphasize the point, the LORD speaks a second time in verse 19, saying, *"They shall fight against you but they shall not prevail... for I am with thee."* In other words, they can't win. This is the LORD's pattern and manner of assurance to those whom He has called. Read Geneses 12:3 where God calls Abraham to leave his home and go to an unknown land. God tells him that *"I will bless them that bless thee, and curse him that curseth thee.* "In Exodus 3: 12, God gives Moses the assurance needed to challenge Pharaoh when the LORD says *"Certainly I will be with Thee."* When God anoints Cyrus to restore Jerusalem, the LORD announces in Isaiah 45:2 that: *"I will go before thee and make the crooked places straight and break in pieces the gates of brass and cut in sunder the bars of iron."* And when the LORD charged Joshua to go over the Jordan, God assures victory in Joshua 1:5 when He says: *"There shall not any man be able to stand before thee all the days of thy life: as I was with Moses, so shall be with thee."* When God Calls, Charges, or Promotes you, He will also prepare the way for you and be with you. The LORD will always give you His Promise and Assurance of Victory as He Stands with you each step of the way.

Prayer:

Father, I thank You for Your Blessed Assurance that allows me to face tomorrow. The charge You've placed in my heart is too daunting for me to take on alone, but hearing Your Voice saying: "I will be with you," makes the load so much lighter. Help me remember that Your Blessed Assurance is better than any insurance I may purchase. Insurance is only powerful after an event occurs; but Your Blessed Assurance is powerful before, during, and after all the events of my life, as they occur. For this I thank You, Father.

In Jesus' Name, Amen.

"If My People, which are called by My Name, shall humble themselves,...then will I Hear from heaven."

Reading;
II Chronicles 7: 11-16

IF ONLY

Scripture;
II Chronicles 7: 11-16

If My People, which are called by My Name, shall humble themselves, and pray, and seek My Face, and turn from their wicked ways; then will I Hear from heaven, and will forgive their sin. and will heal their land. (15) Now Mine Eyes shall be open, and Mine Ears attend unto the prayer that is made in this place."

King James Version

As we stop to take a look at life around us, we sometimes wonder where to turn for direction and hope. We see starvation in Africa and wars in every corner of the globe. School yards and city streets have become war zones, and we have a greater fear that the youth of our families will be buried before the elderly members of our families. There are problems and worries in our lives: there is sickness, confusion, pain, suffering, and disillusionment that we must deal with on a daily basis.

If only we could find that certain something that could wipe away this darkness. That could change these conditions, that could save this lost, confused, and hopeless generation. If only we had the wonder pill, the magic word, the amazing technology that could bring us peace. Oh, how wonderful, Oh, how fantastic, how marvelous life would be! But the question that continually preoccupies our thoughts is: Why must life be so difficult, filled with so much suffering, so much pain, so much trouble? It's times like these that we search for a special leader, for a new way, and a new direction. But we don't need a new hope. What we need is a new look at God, who has been our Hope and Shelter from the beginning of time itself.

In our reading we find king Solomon having the consecration ceremony for the sacred Temple which had just been completed. King Solomon ordered an orchestra of over 120 priests to play and sing. He had an uncountable number of sheep and oxen sacrificed for this occasion. During the celebration He fell to his knees and stretched out his hands and prayed to the LORD. The Bible says that the king prayed, "Oh, LORD my God, if a man sins against his neighbor and comes to this, Your Altar, and asks for forgiveness please hear his cry. And if Your People were defeated in war because they sinned against You, but came back to You, came into Your House of Prayer and asked to be forgiven, please hear their prayer. If there is famine, sickness, or blight in our land and we come into Your House of Prayer, will Thou forgive us of our sins and heal our land?" After he prayed, lightning came down from heaven and consumed the burnt offerings and sacrifices. The Spirit of the LORD filled the Temple, and those who where there gave praises to God's Name. Then king Solomon held a feast for seven days, and on the eighth day he sent the crowd of people home. But that night, as he slept, while it was quiet and still, the LORD came to Solomon saying that He had chosen this house to be His House of Sacrifice. So when the rains of life comes; when the storms of life blow, when the hurricanes and earthquakes of life come; when the diseases and sickness of life come, and His People pray, turn to Him in this house, He will answer. When cancer and confusion come; when aids and arthritis, high blood pressure and MS come. When misunderstandings and misfortunes come, and they pray, He will answer. *"If My People, which are called by My Name shall humble themselves and pray ....I will Hear from heaven and will forgive their sin, and will heal their land."* God is saying if only we would turn from trusting in our own man-made gods and turn back to the one true living God, He would heal our foolish thinking. God says if we would turn to His House of Prayer and turn away from our sins, He will hear our prayers.

I heard a preacher say: "Sin is to honor that which is condemned by God and to detest that which glorifies God. Sin is to place on the throne of life what should be on the footstool of life." God says to turn from our sins, seek His Face and pray, and He will heal our world. If we turn to Him, He will be our support when we are weak, He'll be the light to the path we take, He'll pick us up when life has knocked us down, He'll feed us when we're hungry, bring peace to our home and joy to our life. Today the LORD is calling for us to seek His Face and pray with a humble heart, and He will hear our prayer and heal our souls.

Prayer:

LORD, today hear us as we pray. Forgive us our wrong thinking and wrong doing, and bring to us the peace of Your Spirit: that we may be healed and made whole.

In Jesus' Name, Amen.

"...*Come Ye blessed of my Father,...*"

Reading;
St. Matthew 25: 31-46

DASH

Scripture;
St. Matthew 25: 34

"Then shall the King say unto them on His right hand, Come, ye blessed Of my Father, inherit the kingdom prepared for you from the foundation of the world;..."
King James Version

Have you ever wondered how you will be remembered? Will you be known for the deeds you've performed, the thoughts you shared, the plans you made, the memories you've created? Will your epitaph speak of your smile or your frown? What truths will you have passed on to others? Will your life be an example of wise living rooted in Christ-like precepts, or a life lived with self-centered actions and a disagreeable demeanor? When others read your tombstone, see your dates of birth and death, what will be whispered about the "dash" that is placed between that represents your time spent here on earth. How are you living your "dash"? Are you using your time for God's glory or only to promote your own story? And what if you are one of those who will never see death, but will be caught up with Christ when He comes again; will your dash say to Christ "For You LORD I've lived, and for You I've searched"? My question today is: How are you living your dash?

The text today actually begins at St. Matthew Chapter 24, verse 3, when the disciples ask Christ what will be the signs of His return and the signs of the end time. This is the beginning of what is called the Olivet Discourse; where Christ begins to give the most important words of prophetic insight since the writings of Daniel. **He first tells us to be watchful**. Listen to Him when He says - there will be nations against nations, kingdoms against kingdoms, famines, pestilence, and earthquakes. He warns us that we, who are believers, will be turned over by governments for punishments and death, that believers will turn on other believers, and hate and betray one another, that lawlessness and cold-hearted love will run wild in every corner of the globe. But most importantly, Christ declares that the gospel will be preached in every nation.

Christ warns that when we see these signs, the end is near. We can't help but see the signs that tell us to prepare for His return. It may not be next week or next year, but Christ is coming soon. Wars and fighting in the Middle-East, sickness and distress in our land, strange weather patterns, cancers, AIDS, illnesses that can't be cured, September II, 200I, crazy people with shoe bombs on planes are all telling us Christ is coming soon. In St. Matthew Chapters 24 and 25, Christ gives us three parables and two illustrations to tell us to be ready. The Parable of the Fig Tree, the Illustration of the Days of

Noah, the Parable of the Ten Virgins, the Illustration of the Two Servants, and the Parable of the Talents, all serve to tell us that no man knows the day nor the hour of His return.

The Illustration of the Two Servants, the Parables of the Ten virgins, and the Parable of the Talents, tell us more than to just look for Christ's return. They also tell us to live each day expecting His returns, in other words, to be Faithful. For the wise servant was found working and was made ruler over his master's goods, the five wise virgins took their oil with them and were ready for the bridegroom. The faithful servants with the five and two talents worked, doubled their talents, and were given much more. But the evil servant got drunk and was cut off, the five foolish virgins failed to bring their oil and were left behind, and the servant with the one talent hid it in the ground, had it taken from him, and was cast into outer darkness. Christ says *"I know thy works, tribulation, and poverty .....be thou faithful until death and I will give thee the crown of life"* (Revelation 2:9-10). Ask yourself which one you are, what you are doing with your time, and how you are living for Christ. What are you doing with your dash?

For it's not enough just to look for Christ, it's not enough to just shake our heads when we see evil on TV and foolishness in our school yards. We, who are the believers and saints, the adopted sons and daughters of the King, must also live for Christ. We must live for Him as **wise and faithful** servants, with our lamps burning, our lights shining, and our hearts and minds stayed on Him. **First Christ warns us to be watchful, then directs us to be faithful and dutiful, and now He asks us to be loving**. You can' t feed hungry bodies, quench thirsty spirits or clothe naked souls on a daily basis without the love of God being present within your soul. The work is too hard, the people are too frustrating, and the temptation to quit is too strong. You can't do it without God's Love in your heart. The Presence of Jesus must dwell in you! Church of God, the LORD is calling on us to **be watchful**, to **be faithful**, and to **be loving**; for the world out there needs what we have in here. We need to have our spirits fed, their minds changed, and our souls touched. We need to know that the **Power** of God can save, that the **Spirit** of God can transform, and that the **Love** of God can heal a sin-sick soul. We've been called and commissioned by Christ to preach the good news to the poor, to heal the broken hearted, to bring sight to the blind, and to set the oppressed free.

In a sermon preached over thirty years ago by my spiritual father in the ministry, Reverend David E. Mitcham, the question was asked: "What are you doing with your dash?" I continue to ask myself this question each day, to remind myself not to waste my time here on earth doing foolish things. I don't know about you but I want to fill my time with loving kindness and good deeds. I want to spend my time here in such a way that I can stand before the Father and say that He gave me five talents and I brought Him back ten. I want to hear the Father say, "Well done thy good and faithful servant, well done." I want to hear Christ say, ...*Come ye blessed of My Father, inherit the kingdom prepared for you from the foundation of the world: for I was hungry and you gave Me meat; I was thirsty and you gave Me drink; I was a stranger and you took Me in; I was naked and you clothed Me;*

I was sick and you visited Me; I was in prison and you came to Me." I want to hear, "Well done!"

Prayer:

LORD, help me live my life for You in such a way that the generations following will say: "Here lived a true servant of the King: watchful, faithful and loving. Let my "dash" shine before men in such a way, that when they look at me, they will see only You. "

In Jesus' Name, Amen.

"...what mean these stones..."

Reading;

Joshua 4:19-24

WHAT MEAN THESE STONES

Scripture;

Joshua 4: 21-22,24

"...when your children shall ask their fathers in times to come, saying. What means these stones? (22) Then ye shall let your children know, saying, Israel came over Jordan on dry land... (24) That all the people of the earth might know the hand of the LORD, that it is mighty: that ye might fear the LORD your God for ever."

King James Version

This may be the day that you will meet with the voice of despair, failure and regret. You may hear the voice at your workplace spoken from a co-worker belittling your skills or from your mate or family telling you that you can' t do what you're already doing. You may hear it spoken within yourself, as you remember all the mistakes and missteps you've made. How you respond to the voice will make all the difference on how you see your future, how you complete your day. Do you reject the words spoken and trust in your beliefs, or do you accept the words spoken and retreat into depression and fear? Often when the voice is loud and the words are strong, you need something that you can see or hold onto in order to clear your thoughts. You may need a symbol that says you are more than what the voices want you to believe, that reminds you of your journey and how you made it to this day: "Stones."

Here in the fourth chapter of Joshua we come to a very special moment in the history of Israel. We see Joshua standing before his people explaining the meaning of a monument just built in Gilgal. Joshua looked at the crowd and said; *"...when your children shall ask their fathers in times to come, saying, What means these stones?* (22) *Then ye shall let your children know, saying, Israel came over Jordan on dry land" (Joshua 4:21-22).* To fully understand the meaning of this significant event, we must go back in time and watch history unfold.

The people were about to enter the Promised Land, described in Genesis 15: 18-21. They had spent four hundred years in slavery and forty years in the wilderness in order to reach this day. Moses, their leader, died, and God anointed Joshua to take his place. They had to go through the Jordan River, trusting that God would work a miracle similar to the one performed by Moses at the Red Sea. The people had to march eight miles from Shithim to Jordan and then wash themselves for sanctification. Then Joshua had the priests take the ark of the covenant and walk ⅗th of a mile in front of the people to lead them into the Jordan River. It was harvest time and the waters were running rampant and strong. The river was already overflowing its banks. A reasonable man would have said that the river was uncrossable, that the people should turn around and give up the fight even before they started. But Joshua was following God's directions; he was following a voice with a higher call. So he told the priests to stand in the middle of the Jordan River and hold the ark of the covenant. As the priests reached the bank of the river, the waters rose up and stood as a great wall on one side. While the rest of the water flowed down to the Dead Sea, the wind created a great dry and dusty path for the people to cross over to Gilgal. It took one full day of walking for all the people to cross, and the priests had to stand in the middle of the Jordan until everyone had cross over. And when the people had passed over, Joshua commanded twelve men, one from each tribe, to each place a stone on his shoulder out of the river bed and carry it to the other side. They set twelve stones in the Jordan River also as memorials to the miracle that they had seen. When the priests walk out the river bed, the waters of the river began to flow and overrun its banks again.

Then Joshua went before the people to tell them the meaning of this moment. He says (21) *"...when your children shall ask their fathers in times to come, saying, What means these stones? (22) Then ye shall let your children know, saying, Israel came over Jordan on dry land ... (24) That all the people of the earth might know the Hand of The LORD, that it is mighty: That ye might fear the LORD your God for ever."* They were to remember these stones when the voices of despair, failure, and regret spoke, to remember the Voice of God as He speaks to Abram in Genesis 15: 1, saying, *"...fear not, ...I am thy Shield, and thy Exceeding Great Reward,"* to remember that they are the people God led through the wilderness with a cloud by day and with a pillar of fire by night, to remember that they are the people who God gave manna from heaven when they were hungry and water from a barren rock when they were thirsty, the people to whom God had said, *"I shall make thee the head, and not the tail; and thou shalt be above only, and thou shalt not be beneath; ..." (Deuteronomy 28:13).* If we build a monument of God's Words and deeds in our hearts, then no matter how loud the other voices may be, they can not drown out the Voice of the LORD.

As God's Children, we should always remember the miracles preformed in our lives. We should erect our own "stones" to remind us that the Hand of the LORD is Mighty, and to commemorate the intervention of God's Hand in our lives. The stones speak to us of His healings of loved ones and of ourselves. They speak of doors opening when others blocked our way. They speak of races run and hills climbed, stones like Joshua 1:5 *"...as I was with Moses, so I will be with thee: I will not fail thee, nor forsake thee."* Stones like 1 John 4:4: *"Ye are of God... and have overcome them: because greater is He that is in you, than he that is in the world."* Stones that remind us that the Hand of the LORD is mighty and that He has not failed us yet.

Prayer:

LORD, help us build a monument in our hearts of Your Word, built with stones that remind us that Your Hand is mighty and when we place our hand in Yours, You will always lead us safely home.

In Jesus' Name, Amen.

"As the Father."

Reading;
Job 42: 1-8

TO SEE GOD

_____

Scripture;
Job 42:5

"I have heard of thee by the hearing of the ear: but now mine eye seeth thee. "

King James Version

When you study the book of Job you see that it is divided into three parts: the prologue, the dialogue, and the epilogue. The prologue is that part that introduces us to Job and the theme of this writing. It tells us that Job was a wealthy man, a man that had every good and precious gift that God could give. He had land and possession, and he had money and respectability. He had family and friends, and he also was a man known for his fear of God and his hatred of evil. The Bible says that he was the greatest of all men in the East. He would wake up every morning and offer burnt offerings for his children just in case they may have offended God overnight by their words, thoughts, or deeds.

The **prologue** also introduces us to the villain of this poetic writing: Satan, and when Satan comes into the picture, everything changes. One day Job was able to sip champagne, knowing that he didn't have a care in the world, and the next day he found himself not even wanting to sip soup because of all the trouble he had to bear. Job is the symbol of great suffering in life, unmerited suffering: suffering not due to his own making, but because of the misdeeds and circumstances of others. First, Satan strikes Job's finances: the Seabeans take his oxen and his mules. The Chaldeans steal his camels, and a storm kills his sheep. Secondly, Satan touches Job's loved ones: that same storm takes the lives of his servants, but worst of all, a second storm destroyed the house of his eldest son and killed all of Job's children as they ate dinner together.

The **dialogue** is the conversation between Job and others who came to be with him during his time of need. Here we can see how Job's troubles affected him. The story goes on to say that the devil touches Job a third time making him physically ill, placing a disease of the skin on him, a disease of boils from the top of his head to the bottom of his feet. It was so bad that even his wife told Job to curse God and die. His friends who had traveled from a faraway land, looked at him; saw his condition but didn't know what to say to him. After seven days of quiet suffering, Job finally begins to speak, cursing his life. Now the dialogue shows us the next area of attack Satan brings: the fourth effect: of being falsely accused, unjustly criticized, and misunderstood by friends and everyone else. His friends began to tell him to repent of the sin that he must have committed for God to have placed all this misery on him. In the midst of this dialogue, Job began to speak out about his pain. His pain was deeper than a physical or psychological pain. It was the deep, devastating soul-wrenching hurt of spiritual pain. Life can get you down; it can be so rough, and so hard, and so confusing that you don't know which way to turn. It can have you thinking that you can't do anything right. You make the folks you love angry because of what you won't do, and you make other folks mad because of the things that you've chosen to do. Like Job, life can make your dreams disappear like a puff of smoke, making you feel that life is not worth living and that you would be better off if you would just sit down and die. You sit and watch those things you hold dear fade away from you, and it seems that you're helpless to do anything about it. And here, Job lies in his bed of affliction, misunderstood by his friends, confused, and weak in spirit.

The **epilogue**: the conclusion in verse, that which brings it all together. It begins with Elihu, a young companion of the three friends of Job. He tells Job that Job has sinned against God by detailing his situations, that if God has not answered him, it's because Job is insincere in his request. Elihu represents those young "know it all" religious folks, (not young in age, but young in spirit), those who received God's Salvation at last Sunday's service and think that all the wisdom of age and time has been placed in their little pea brain. They think that they can speak for God and that because they've read a book, they're now theologians and prophets. They think that only their religious experience is real, that everyone else is lost without them and their knowledge. They're so busy beating you with their Bibles that they fail to encourage you with God's Words of loving kindness, peace, and comfort. They are the ones that Paul speaks to when he says: *"Though I speak with the tongue of men and of angels, and have not love I am become as sounding brass, or a tinkling cymbal, And though I have the gift of prophecy and understand all mysteries and all knowledge; and though I have all faith, so that I could remove mountains and have not love I am nothing."* (*1 Corinthians 13:1-2*). Elihu was a religious follower without a relationship: religious followers without a relationship are like poles, they only reach up to touch God, not seeking vision or purpose. Followers with a relationship are more like the cross: on their vertical axis they reach up to touch the Hand of God and His Loving Kindness, but on their horizontal axis they reach out to spread the Love of God demonstrating His Grace and Mercy.

The epilogue **first teaches us** how to treat our friends in times of trouble. The Bible says God tells Job's friends that what they did was wrong, that instead of chastising Job, they should have talked with him in prayer. Instead of accusing Job, they should have trusted in God and told the LORD of their love for Job, their friend. **Secondly**, it teaches us that we've got to know God personally, because it was after Job could say: *"... but now mine eye seeth thee."* that he was able to understand God's Divine nature. It was within this moment that Job's personal suffering and pain turned into redemptive suffering. Chapter 42 verse 10, says that God turned Job's situation around when he prayed for his friends. He prayed for them even while he was sick and suffering, while still in his bed of afflictions. Job's new sight allows him to pray and reach out for the salvation of someone else. He now has a new vision and a new understanding of everything around him, so much so that he can pray for those who misunderstood him, criticized, and looked down on him. Verse ten also says that after he prayed for his friends, God gave Job twice as much as he had before. God will bless our pain and make it bear fruit; He will reward our faithfulness, allowing us to reach higher levels in Him, if only we surrender our hearts and wills into His Spirit. So what is our lesson for today? It is this: when you find friends who are down because of what life has done to them, don't try to give them your philosophy or tell them about your religion. Don't knock them down with your Bible, but lift them up with your prayers. Don't talk about them; pray about them. Don't tell them about the sins they've committed or the good they've failed to do. Don't tell them that they're sick because of something they did long, long ago. If you want to help them, if you truly care for them, if you want the best for them, then all you need to do is: "Pray for them." Support them with your love!

Pray that they may be what God wants them to be and that they may see what God wants for them to see, that they may see God with new spiritual eyes so that they may know Him in a new way. Pray, calling out their name. Pray, asking God to reach down and touch them, to heal them, to speak the words that will transform their mind, heart, and soul, and give them His Peace.

Prayer:

LORD, help me to see You with new eyes, so that I might see others with a new compassion, a compassion that allows me to pray for others in the midst of my pain and to lead them to You.

In Jesus' Name, Amen.

As the Father hath loved Me, so have I loved you: continue ye in My love."

Reading;

St. John 15: 1-14

THIS IS MY COMMANDMENT

Scripture;

St. John 15: 12

"This is My commandment, That ye love one another, as I have loved you. "

King James Version

The last hours spent with a loved ones are both memorable and precious, You remember your last conversation together; their last instructions, questions, or blessings spoken to you. I remember the last week spent with my best friend before his death, our last dialogue and parting words. I remember the last words said by my father before he passed. I recall vividly the last song sung by my mother days before her transition. Most dear to me still, are the words of my grandmother, words of encouragement and exhortation. From her hospital bed she instructed me to continue to "Preach The Word." A moment in time that is as fresh to me today as it was in August of 1986, the day they were spoken. Here in St. John Chapter 15, we witness Christ speaking to His closest friends important last words of instructions and comfort.

In St. John 12:23 Jesus says: *"...the hour is come, that the Son of man should be glorified."* Christ is preparing them for His crucifixion and the events that will follow. He has only a few hours to be with them, and He wants them to understand the most important thoughts of His Heart. Jesus has given them power to cast out devils, heal the sick, cleanse lepers, and raise the dead. He has shown them miracles, signs, and wonders and has elevated them from students to friends. Now He prepares them for His last walk, His final hour. He speaks to them of their relationship to Him and His relationship to the Father. He speaks of His Love for the Father, theirs for Him, and His for them. So Christ says: *(9) As the Father hath loved Me, so have I loved you: continue ye in My Love. (10) ye keep My Commandments, ye shall abide in My Love; even as I have kept My Father's Commandments, and abide in His Love" (St. John 15:9-10).* Christ speaks of "agape" love, a love that is totally sacrificial and unconditional for God. Agape love implores you to reach out to others, in spite of your differences. Agape love is not a feeling but a decision, a decision to choose to help others, not to hinder them. Agape love means you choose to feed the hungry, give a cold glass of water to the thirsty, and visit the sick-not because it feels good, but because of the call to be faithful to the God you serve. And Christ in His final hours, tells His disciples three times to "love one another" (St. John 13:34; 15:12; 15:17).

He taught them of death, suffering and, forgiveness. faith, prayer, and righteousness, but Jesus says; *"This is My Commandment, that ye love one another, as if have loved you."* It takes agape love to walk the extra mile with a friend, to turn the other cheek and to forgive men who trespassed against you. It takes agape to love your enemies, to bless them that curse you, to do good to them that hate you or to pray for them that despise you. But Jesus says, to be His disciples, that is what we must do. When His "hour had come," Christ wanted those closest to Him to remember to love one another above all the other lessons He taught. That was most important. When my "hour comes," I pray that I would have lived in such a way that my loved ones can look at my life and remember these words: "Love one another as I have loved you," and that they will choose to reach out, love, and bless others the way Christ loved us.

Prayer:

Father, teach us how to love with an agape love: choosing to reach out to others, no matter our differences. Then teach us to live our lives so that others will choose to love as we have loved.

In Jesus' Name, Amen.